D0646788

HEAVYWEIGHTS

THE MILITARY USE OF MASSIVE WEAPONS

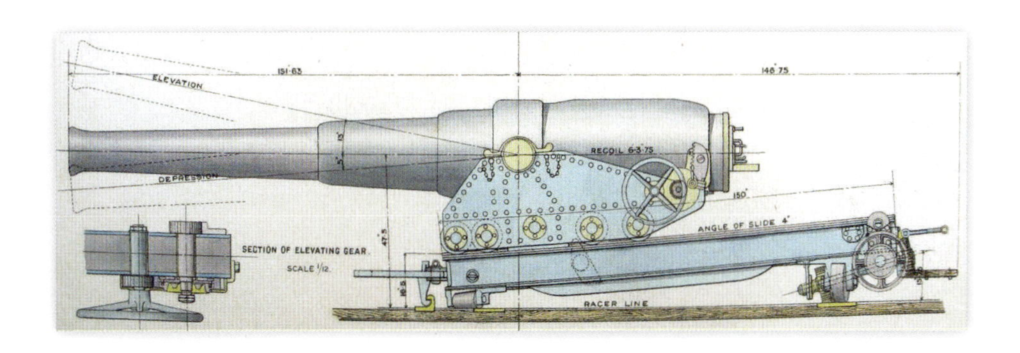

HEAVYWEIGHTS

THE MILITARY USE OF MASSIVE WEAPONS

LEO MARRIOTT &
JONATHAN FORTY

CHARTWELL
BOOKS

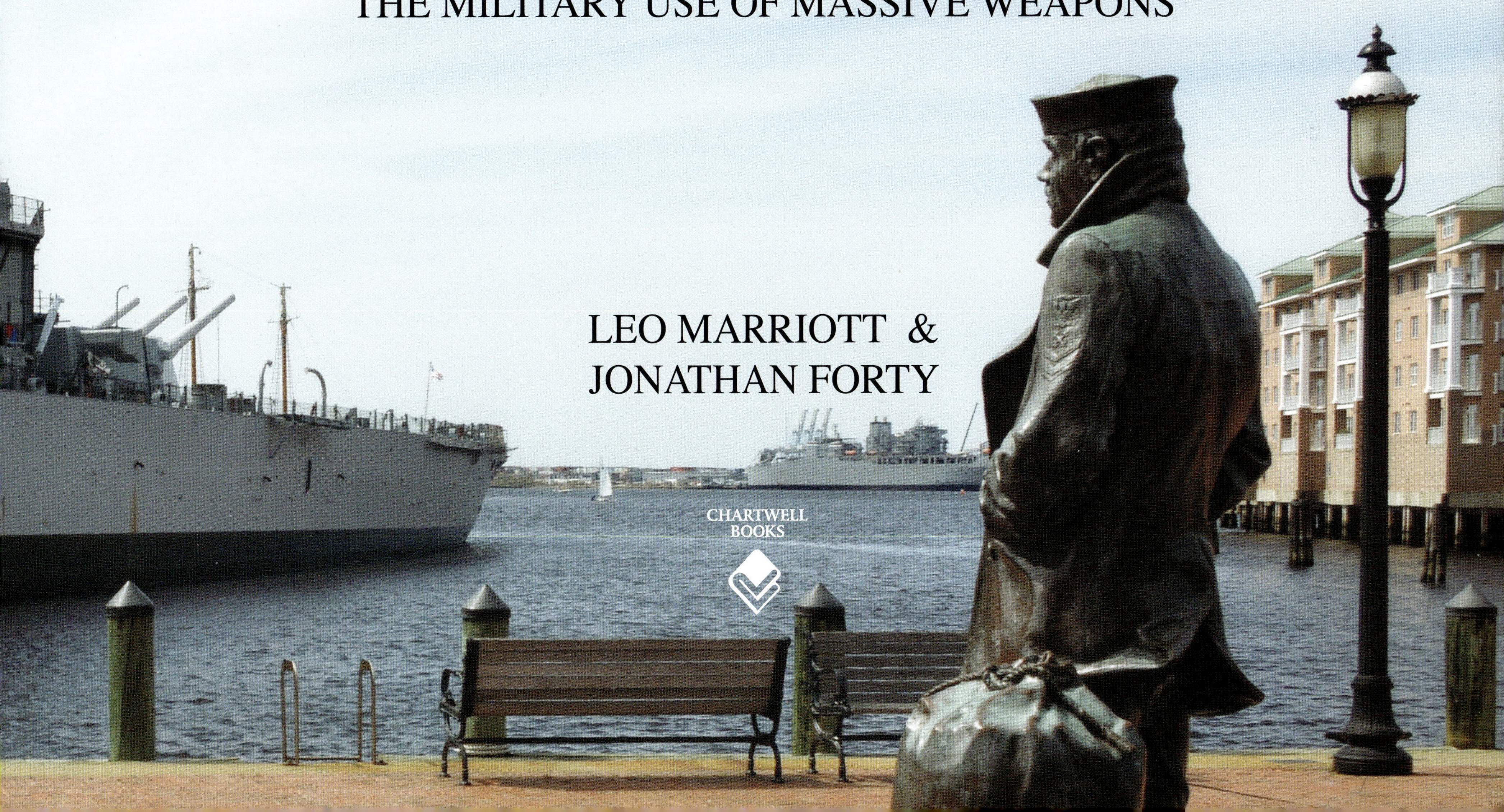

This edition published in 2017 by Chartwell Books
an imprint of The Quarto Group
142 West 36th Street, 4th Floor
New York, NY 10018 USA
T (212) 779-4972 F (212) 779-6058
www.QuartoKnows.com

ISBN: 978-0-7858-3549-3

Printed and bound in China

10 9 8 7 6 5 4 3 2 1

Design: Greene Media Ltd/EF Design

Page 1: *Diagram of a British BL 8-inch 12-ton gun on a naval carriage.*

Pages 2/3: *"Iowa" class battleship USS* Wisconsin, *today a museum ship, is berthed at Norfolk, VA . Its main armament is nine 16-inch (410 mm)/50 cal Mk. 7 guns in three turrets. Reactivated for the Gulf War* Wisconsin *received four launchers for AGM-84 Harpoon anti-ship missiles, eight mounts for BGM-109 Tomahawk missiles, and four of the USN's Phalanx Close in Weapon System CIWS) 20mm Gatling guns for defense against enemy anti-ship missiles and enemy aircraft.*

This Page: *16-inch howitzer M1920 stamped "Watervliet Arsenal 1921," Fort Story, VA, 1942.*

Contents

Glossary and Abbreviations

AP armor-piercing
ALVF *l'Artillerie Lourds sur Voie Ferrée*—French heavy rail artillery
barbette Initially a circular open armored structure aboard a warship in which heavy guns were mounted. Subsequently the guns were protected by an armored turret which rotated over the fixed barbette
caliber (cal) The diameter of the bore of a gun barrel. Also used as a unit of length of a gun barrel. For example a 10-inch/20-cal gun would have a barrel 200 inches long (10 x 20). This is specified in millimeters, centimeters, or inches depending on the historical period and national preference
BL breech-loader
cascable The casting at the rear of a muzzle-loading cannon
chevaux de frise defensive anti-cavalry measure: a portable frame or log covered with projecting spikes
CSS Confederate States Ship
cwt hundredweight: unit of Imperial weight equal to 112lb
E *Eisenbahnlafette* (railroad car gun-mount) or *Eisenbahnartillerie* (railroad artillery)
EMRG electromagnetic railgun
First rate Starting in the 17th century RN ships of the line were rated to differentiate ships considered suitable for various functions. By the 18th century First Rate ships carried 100 guns and nearly 1,000 crew. Fifth and Sixth Rate were frigates
FOO Foward observation officer
gabion a cage, cylinder, or box filled with rocks, concrete, or sometimes sand and soil; often used to protect artillery
GPS global positioning system
GRAU Missile and Artillery Directorate of the Ministry of Defense of the Russian Federation
HARP High Altitude Research Project
Haubitze howitzer (German)
HE high explosive
HMS His/Her Majesty's ship
IED improvised explosive device
ML muzzle-loader
Mle *Modèle* (model)

Below: *Diagram 1: Trajectories. Artwork on this spread by* Mark Franklin.

Opposite, Above: *Diagram 2: Railway gun mounts (a) and recoil systems (b).*

Opposite, Below: *Diagram 3: Parts of a cannon.*

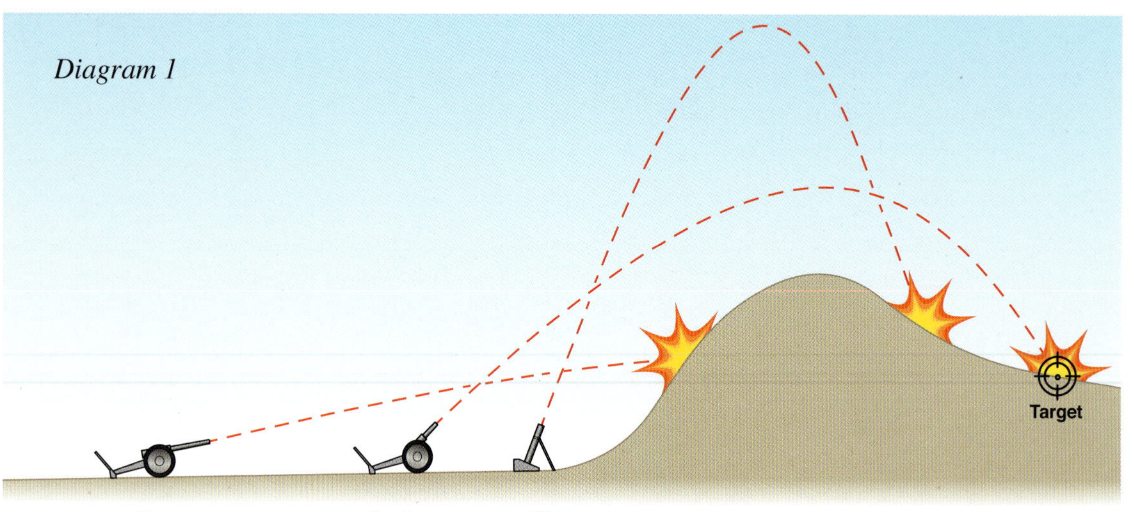

MKB *Marine Küsten Batterie* German Navy coastal battery
MLR muzzle-loading rifle
MLRS multi-launch rocket system
MRSI multiple rounds simultaneous impact
Panzerschiff(e) armored ship(s)
pdr pounder
psi pounds per square inch
railroad gun recoil systems see diagram 2:

- cradle—the gun recoils backward in its cradle, retarded and stopped by hydraulic buffers
- top-carriage—the gun is mounted in an upper carriage that moves on wheels on fixed rails
- sliding—the car body sits on a set of wooden crossbeams placed underneath it which have been jacked down on to a special set of girders incorporated into the track. The gun, car body, and trucks all recoil together with the friction generated by the crossbeams sliding on the girders absorbing the recoil force
- rolling—the entire gun, mount and everything rolls backward

RBL rifled breech-loader
RGA Royal Garrison Artillery
RHA Royal Horse Artillery
RML rifled muzzle-loader
RN Royal Navy
SK C *Schnelladekanone* (quick-loading cannon); C - *Construktionsjahr* (year of design)—German gun designations
TLP *très longue portée* (very long range)
TOT time on target
trajectory see diagram 1
USS United States ship

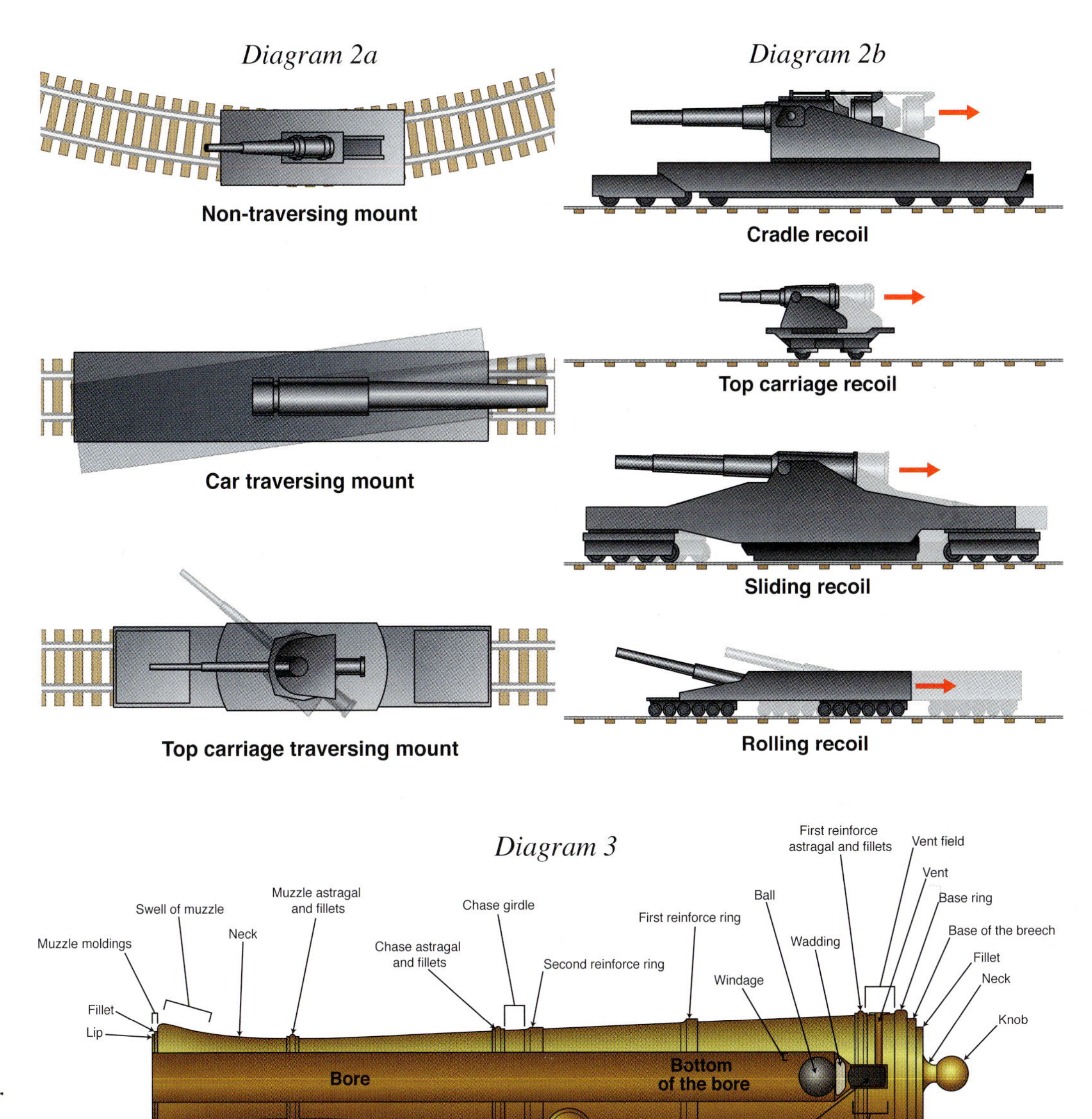

Introduction

Below: *From the start, the military has tried to maximize the range and effect of guns. With cannon it was not just a case of firing a big shot: spread and weight of anti-personnel fire was also important—hence the development of shrapnel and the use of multiple barrels. Early 16th-century Ottoman multi-barreled volley gun.*

Opposite, Above: *Cannon on the bastion of St. Rocha defending the Polish fortress of Jasna Gora from Swedish siege in 1655.*

Opposite, Below: *The longevity of cannon is remarkable. This Ottoman example was made on October 8, 1581 and was seized in 1830 at Algiers.*

The introduction of gunpowder and the creation of firearms introduced a new paradigm to warfare, one that would go on to have deep and far-reaching consequences for human technological development. The exploitation of chemical energy to fire ranged weapons was to radically change the balance of power on the battlefield, making castles and armor virtually obsolete and the professional and individual skill of the knight almost irrelevant, thus also contributing significantly to social change and the demise of the feudal system. Its use would force the creation of new types of troops to use the new weapons, with new formations and new tactics which have led, in a relatively short time, to the modern armies of today.

Delivering the heaviest possible munitions onto the enemy and his strongpoints serves a number of military functions: it destroys protective positions and so is ideal for siege or trench warfare; it kills and maims at a distance without endangering one's own troops or provides devastating close-range protection against attack; also significant, it saps the enemy's morale as it searches them out far from the front lines, degrading their performance and reducing their maneuverability.

Despite the difficulty of historical records and lack of hard archeology what can be said is that the Chinese, having invented gunpowder and used it in their inter-state wars against each other, reached a degree of sophistication beginning with fireworks and "fire lances," through rockets, grenades and bombs to guns—cast bronze metal weapons firing projectiles. Their use spread swiftly west and as it did so new developments began to appear, with its the adoption firstly by the Mongols and then with the spread of Islam to the emerging Muslim states. Sometimes known as the Gunpowder Empires, the first and foremost were the Ottomans. Bayazid I besieged and took Salonica using heavy siege guns in 1430 and Mehmet II famously took Byzantium in 1453; Selim I conclusively won the battle of Chaldiran against the rival Safavids in 1514 with a mixture of cannon and musketry. The Ottoman Janissaries were the first professional firearm-equipped military unit in the world. The Persian Safavids learned from their heavy defeat and also began arming their troops with guns and using cannon. The Mughals had learned from the Mongols and in 1526 Babur conquered the Delhi Sultanate at the battle of Panipat using muskets and cannon.

While in the East these large Islamic empires held sway, Europe, being geographically smaller, was more compact and cellular with the necessary metal-working skills spread across the continent, not concentrated in the power of a single state. The Renaissance (c. 1300–1700) and Reformation (c. 1517–1648) spurred on much social, political, and industrial change and local competitive conditions were ripe for a developmental surge in the sciences and manufacturing. As the European states became more advanced and sophisticated, so too did their armies and weapons, and Europe soon became the center of gun development. Gunpowder, too, being costly and time consuming to produce until rich mineral sources of nitrates were discovered, was as valuable as the cannon themselves. There was a major improvement when a new wet-grinding process was developed. This produced a paste that when dry was "corned"—diced into small lumps which produced a consistent and more powerful explosive blast.

Cannon were at first cast in bronze, later iron, and then steel. The largest were used in sieges and seacoast defenses and on warships. These included the German mortar—a chunky, thick-walled and short-barreled gun that fired at a steep angle to blast walls or bombard targets behind them. At sea, cannon were the only weapons that could splinter the massive wooden walls of warships in the days of sail, and sea battles continued to see huge weapons employed

continued on p. 13

Left: *Detail from Hans Hrell's painting of the battle of Orsha, fought on September 8, 1514, showing Polish artillery crossing the River Krapivna. The sizable Russian force attacked the Lithuanian and Polish forces but were defeated, with the artillery playing a significant role. Painted c. 1524–1530, it now resides in the National Museum, Warsaw.*

Right: *Braun and Hogenberg's map of Antwerp from* Civitates Orbis Terrarum *shows the way that fortifications had changed over the 16th century as a result of gunpowder and siege weapons. Note the star-shaped citadel in this map published in 1572 and the angled city walls. These were so designed to allow defensive cannon to have interlocking fields of fire against attackers.*

through to World War II: the 460mm guns of the "Yamato" class or the 16-inch guns of the "Iowa" class battleships could engage the enemy at twenty-four miles, and the latter saw service into the 1990s. It was only the advent of carrier-based aviation that saw the end of the huge battleships and their strategic importance.

The threat of invasion from the sea saw coastline countries develop more and more sophisticated state-sponsored seacoast defenses—some of the last castles to be built. Rather than high towers and thin curtain walls they became low turrets squatting behind elaborate thick berm earthen walls, faced and revetted with stone. These defenses evolved to cope with increasingly powerful munitions from the star forts of Vauban through thick stone-fronted gun bastions excavated into cliffs or built into other natural features to the massive metal-reinforced concrete sunken bunker complexes of Hitler's Atlantic Wall. Often these defenses were equipped with naval guns taken from decommissioned or unbuilt battleships.

A quantum leap in weapons' development came with Europe and America's Industrial Revolution (1760–1840), which saw substantial advances in the fields of metallurgy, chemistry, and engineering. New more powerful propellants and improved metal-working magnified the destructive capability of new weapons. Iron gave way to steel and smoothbore muzzle-loaders gave way to rifled breech-loaders, with hydro-pneumatic recoil systems that absorbed the blast force and returned the weapon automatically to its firing position, ensuring stability and continuity of fire. Wooden warships became metal and munitions changed from solid round shot through canister shrapnel shot to cylindroconic shells with armor-piercing capability. (A gun is described by caliber—its bore diameter, specified in millimeters, centimeters, or inches depending on the

Opposite: *Battery Oldenburg, part of the German offensive capability at "Hellfire Corner" the closest point between France and the UK. Initially armed with 210mm guns in 1940, latterly two casemates were constructed. They housed Russian guns that were rechambered by Krupp to 240mm. The coastal guns around the Pas de Calais were strikingly ineffective: of the thousand rounds fired only two ships were sunk, both in 1944.*

Left: *Citadel Hill (Fort George) gunpowder magazine. The Museum of Naval Firepower created within 18th century buildings at the Royal Navy's former armaments depot of Priddy's Hard, in Gosport, England is appropriately named Explosion! Appropriately not just for the concussive effect of big naval guns but because of the immediate result of a mistake by munitions' workers, or enemy fire reaching a magazine like this one in Halifax, Nova Scotia, Canada.*

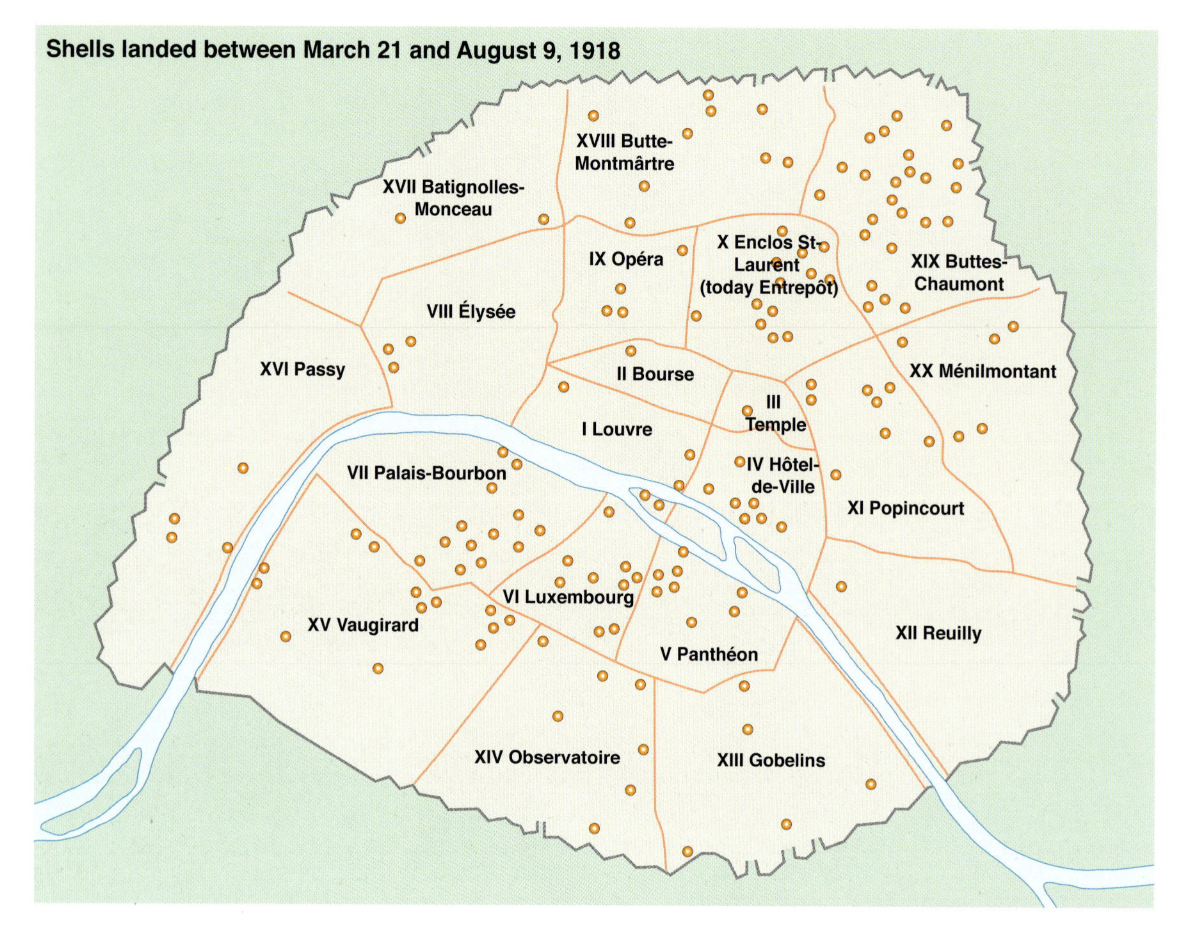

historical period and national preference.) Technological advances also included the continued refinement of barrel rifling as it was found that a gyroscopic spin on a fired shell increased its range, stability, and accuracy. The old black powder propellant was replaced with a series of more powerful explosives discovered virtually simultaneously in different parts of Europe—gun cotton made from nitrocellulose, nitroglycerin, dynamite, gelignite, and cordite. As the quality and range of artillery increased, the exact time of detonation became more vital leading to the development of fuses of different duration from air burst to immediate contact. Sights, elevation, and traverse mechanisms also became more sophisticated.

With the ever-growing destructive capacity of heavy weapons, all key installations became increasingly protected—often subterranean—and defenses more ergonomic to disguise their appearance from observation. Cities themselves could not hide and bore the brunt of long-range bombardment as artillery was used as a terror weapon—for example, Paris was bombarded during 1871 by the Germans, killing over 400 civilians—and then again in 1918 when the German Paris guns bombarded the city firing on a parabola through the stratosphere.

Above: *In 1918, the three Paris guns fired around 367 rounds, 183 of which landed within the city. Casualties were 250 dead and 620 wounded.*

Right: *The* Katyusha *multiple rocket launcher was first built and fielded by the Soviet Union in World War II.*

The use of artillery en masse on a battlefield saw an increase in range beyond line of sight to that of indirect fire. This in turn lead to the development of range-finding and targeting using increasingly complicated equipment beginning with targeting tables and ending with computers. With time and experience the triangulation of reconnaissance, observation and targeting enabled predictive fire that factored range precisely.

The 20th century witnessed the two largest wars to date, with a surge in artillery development leading to the colossal—often railroad—superguns used to bombard targets from long distances. In World War 2, the *Nebelwerfer* and *Katushya* rocket launchers were new versions of an ancient weapon originally used by the Chinese and the Mughals and later updated by Congreve. They are still in use today as the MLRS (Multi-Launch Rocket System). However, by the end of that century air power and the arrival of missile technology signaled the decline of the supergun. First the airship and then the long-range bomber transferred the onus of attacking distant targets to the air forces, though they too were somewhat invalidated in turn by the development of nuclear weapons and intercontinental ballistic missile technology.

In the late 1970s precision munitions had started to appear that tracked a laser designator which identified the target precisely. Other early 21st century military inventions that benefit us all include the necklace of satellites around the Earth that enable GPS—a system that can be used to guide anything accurately anywhere, including shells and missiles. The introduction of these new systems led to a necessity for very accurate three-dimensional target coordinates. Command and Control uses communications and intelligence to detect, identify and acquire targets in order to allocate resources and achieve mission success. Mobile and man-portable radio and computer communications are an essential component to assimilate and connect all the different elements of a combat mission. Information is gathered from satellites, drones, aircraft, laser rangefinders, ground surveillance radars, night vision equipment, flash and sound sensors and even human FOOs. With this combination of image intelligence), signals intelligence, electronic intelligence, and human intelligence) accurate firing data is computed and sent to the selected gun units, along with logistical support providing equipment, ammunition and supplies. Ammunition is assigned according to the target need, with a choice of three basic types—bursting and base or nose ejection.

The final hurrah of the supergun was the Space Gun designed by Gerald Bull, who was head-hunted by Iraqi dictator Saddam Hussein to build an even bigger super-gun (Big Babylon—see p. 219) that did not reach completion before he was assassinated. Though still a vital battlefield asset, the days off the super-large bombard appear, for now, to be over.

Right: *The V-3 was a supergun that worked on the multi-charge principle. The test ground was the island of Wolin, and the weapon is seen here in 1943.*

Naval Weapons

Right: *Veronese's* Battle of Lepanto *in the Accademia of Venice. On October 7, 1571, Turkish naval pretensions in the Mediterranean were dealt a significant blow by the navy of the Holy League, under the command of Don John of Austria. Lepanto had a further significance: it was the last major battle fought almost entirely between galleys. (Indeed, the freed Christian galley slaves of the Turks played a major role in the battle.) One of the reasons for the Christians' success was their artillery which was superior in numbers, ammunition, and capability to the Turks.*

Opposite: *Carl Frederik Sørensen's* Sea Battle at Lissa.

The invention of gunpowder and its consequent application to projectile weapons rapidly changed the nature of warfare, not only on land but also at sea. Traditionally ships were merely a means of transporting troops and soldiers who, if they came into contact with an enemy vessel, would attempt to overcome it by grappling alongside and boarding. As the vessels approached each other volleys of arrows might be exchanged but the outcome was decided by hand-to-hand combat—much the same as a land battle but fought on floating platforms. Early exceptions to this were the use of oar-propelled vessels equipped with sharp and heavy ram bows capable of sinking an enemy vessel—perhaps the original heavyweight weapon. In fact oar-propelled galleys were widely used by Mediterranean nation states and survived until well into the 18th century. However, the use of such ships was problematic and depended heavily on the particular conditions and tactics of the time although it is worth noting that steam-driven ram vessels were briefly popular in the latter half of the 19th century following the success of the Austrian fleet under Admiral Tegetthoff which inflicted a heavy defeat on an Italian fleet at the Battle of Lissa in 1866. Ramming tactics played a significant role in the sinking of two Italian ironclads.

In medieval times there were no permanent navies or specialized warships (apart from the Mediterranean war galleys). Those vessels engaged in wars were basically merchant ships adapted to carry soldiers and often fitted with structures over the bow and stern which acted as strongpoints and gave positions from which archers could shoot down at an enemy. When early guns became available in the 14th century they were often mounted in these "castles" and

initially were light anti-personnel weapons (colloquially known as "murderers") and not capable of causing any significant damage to an enemy ship. However, as metal working and foundry techniques improved, heavier weapons were introduced in the 15th century. Mounting these in turn demanded substantial modifications to the ships that carried them, so they were no longer suitable for mercantile work and the concept of the sailing warship was born.

On land artillery evolved along two distinct lines of development. Armies in the field needed weapons which could be transported and brought into action on the battlefield. As they were reliant on teams of horses for movement there was a practical limit to the size of field pieces but this restriction did not apply guns mounted in forts, castles, and other prepared positions. Here would be found the larger and more powerful cannons. However the situation at sea was different as once a piece was mounted in a ship it was instantly capable of mobility at sea. As ships grew larger they could carry more and heavier weapons. For over 300 years from the early 16th to the middle of the 19th century there was little significant change in the design of ships and their armament and the largest vessels could carry a hundred or more guns arranged in three tiers or decks. This allowed a broadside of 50 heavy cannon from a single ship—a concentration of firepower which could never be matched on land. Of course such fire was generally directed at other ships and was rarely employed against land targets due to the relatively short range of the muzzle-loading cannon firing solid round shot. In any case it was generally accepted that it was not worthwhile for a ship to engage a well-constructed and heavily armed fort although such engagements did take place with varying results.

Technical advances in the 19th century completely altered naval gunnery. In the 1820s the French general Henri-Joseph Paixhans invented and successfully demonstrated an explosive shell which could be fired from high-powered naval guns. The idea was quickly adopted and by the 1840s all major navies employed such weapons which were capable of wreaking havoc aboard the contemporary wooden warships. A further advance was the introduction of rifling to the barrels of the muzzle-loading guns which considerably improved their accuracy, especially when the cylindroconical projectiles were introduced. The drawback of such weapons was the increased difficulty of loading and quite complex equipment was required to achieve this as the weight of projectiles rose from the standard 32-pdr of Nelson's navy to larger 68-pdrs and 110-pdrs and ultimately a 16-inch caliber MLR firing a 1,684lb shell. At that stage an efficient hydraulic loading mechanism had been developed.

The final advance was the invention of the interrupted screw as a simple method of sealing the firing chamber in breech-loading guns and this was widely adopted by navies from the 1870s onwards. A major disadvantage of the muzzle-loading gun was that the barrel need to be relatively short so that it could be accessed by the loading mechanism but this restriction was lifted by the introduction of breech-loaders. With longer rifled barrels made of steel rather than iron, naval guns could achieve much greater ranges with increased accuracy. Since the end of the 19th century the basic design of naval heavy guns has remained much the same although calibers steadily increased from a standard 12-inch to the 15 and 16-inch guns widely used in World War II (and even 18-inch in the case of the Japanese navy).

In the era of muzzle-loading cannon and wooden sailing ships, most engagements were fought at close range where rate of fire was more important than accuracy. However, the advent of shell-firing guns with long rifled barrels rapidly increased attainable ranges making accurate fire much more

Opposite: *HMS* Victory *is simply a floating gun platform. The major decision relating to the design of any warship was the number of guns she would carry. Once this was set—in* Victory*'s case at 100—the division of guns on each gun deck could be worked out, and the dimensions of the ship derived at. To emphasize the importance of the gun to a warship such as* Victory, *it's worth remembering that at Trafalgar, she carried 104 guns over four decks. The British army fielded 161 in total at Waterloo. The weight of fire was huge:* Victory*'s first broadside at Trafalgar weighed 1.25 tons!*

Opposite, Above: *Looking down the barrels of a pair of 12-inch guns on HMS* Dreadnought*—two of a homogeneous battery of ten such guns carried by the first modern warship. They dwarf the pair of QF 12-pounder anti-torpedo boat guns mounted on the turret roof.*

Opposite, Below: *The battlecruiser HMS* Hood *was launched on August 22, 1918 and was the largest and most powerful warship in the world with a top speed of 32 knots. That was not the case on May 24, 1941, when she faced the Nazi ~~pocket~~ battleship* Bismarck *in the Denmark Strait, still with the same armor. Plunging fire ignited the* Hood*'s aft magazine and only three of the 1,421 men on board survived.*

difficult. Initially adjustable sights were installed on each gun mounting with a sightsetter being an additional member of the gun crew. However, as distances increased empirical estimates of ranges were not good enough and optical rangefinders were introduced to give more accurate ranges which could be transmitted to the sightsetter by telephone or by visual pointers or counters. Each gun was still controlled and fired independently which made it difficult to apply corrections by spotting the fall of shot, a situation aggravated by the fact that until 1905 all battleships carried a variety of different caliber guns. One of the lessons drawn from the battle of Tushima (1904) was the relative ineffectiveness of this type of shooting. The solution to this problem was clearly demonstrated by the Royal Navy when it launched HMS *Dreadnought* in 1905 whose main armament was a homogeneous battery of ten 12-inch guns. In addition the concept of salvo firing where all the guns fired simultaneously made spotting the fall of shot much easier. Salvoes also overcame the fact that, no matter how accurately aimed, the performance of individual guns would vary slightly but with eight or ten shells fired together the spread of shot would tend to cancel out individual errors and increase the chance of a hit.

A ship such as *Dreadnought* could steam at twenty-one knots and fire at ranges up to 20,000 yards and could be faced with engaging a target moving at a similar speed on a different course. Even if an accurate range and bearing could be measured the shell would take over half a minute to reach the target which in that time would have moved by several hundred yards. The calculations necessary to take account of the many factors involved were extremely complex and well beyond any manual solution. In the early part of the 20th century this led to the development of some quite sophisticated electro-mechanical analog computers. Among the earliest was a device known as a "Dumaresq" (named after its inventor Lt. Dumaresq, RN). Essentially, it was a set of interlocking circular slide rules which could calculate rate of change of range and bearing, these results then being applied to an aiming offset allowing for time of flight of the shell. Another device was a range clock which, based on constant range updates, would produce a forecast range for any period ahead. Subsequently, the principles involved in these devices were incorporated into the Dreyer Fire Control Table which became standard in British battleships during World War I. This, in turn, was replaced by the Admiralty Fire Control Table which, in various formats, provide fire control solutions for a range of warships until eventually superseded by modern digital computers.

The other significant development which was incorporated in British warships just prior to World War I was director firing. Instead of the output from the fire control systems being fed individually to each gun, it was now passed though a central director positioned high up on the ship with a good view of the action and its own rangefinder. The director could then apply any last minute adjustments and control the actual firing of the guns to ensure accurate salvo fire. Other navies developed similar systems which differed slightly in terms of operational practice to achieve the same effect.

As artillery developed in the latter half of the 19th century, naval gunnery faced a problem which did not affect land-based artillery to any great extent. As warships began to be constructed of metal and were protected by ever-thickening layers of armor plate it was necessary to develop projectiles which could penetrate such armor before exploding in order to cause the maximum amount of damage. Initially armor comprised thicker and thicker sheets of iron plate as the weight and size of projectiles increased: by 1873 HMS *Inflexible* armed with 16-inch MLR had an armored citadel protected by up to 24 inches of armor. This was more than the practical limit as the weight of the armor severely handicapped the design and functioning of the ship. However from 1877 new forms of armor using hardened steel plate came into use and this was both stronger and lighter. Even so, battleships of all nations in World War I and II were protected by 12–16 inches of armor covering vital areas such as magazines, gun turrets and machinery spaces.

The ability of a shell to penetrate such armor depended on its weight and the velocity at which it hit its target. Larger shells had greater kinetic energy and consequently did not slow down in flight as much as lighter shells and this was the main reason that gun calibers continued to increase. Another factor was the angle at which the armor plate was struck. For example if struck at degrees from the normal the effective thickness of the armor is increased and in the case of the British 15-inch gun it would only penetrate nine inches of armor but could defeat sixteen inches if struck at an angle of only five degrees. In order to achieve the smaller angles it was necessary to engage at a relatively short range. This was one reason why in May 1941 Vice Admiral Holland aboard HMS *Hood* was eager to reduce the range before turning on to a parallel course to the *Bismarck*.

The reverse was true of deck armor where the best effects were achieved by plunging fire at long range. As this decreased the shell would strike at a shallower angle and at some point be unable to penetrate. It would then by necessary to shorten the range to a point where the flatter trajectory would enable the side armor to be penetrated. This led to a theoretical "invulnerability zone" in which a ship should be able to withstand hits from armor-piercing shells.

By end of World War II, in 1945 the big-gun battleship was obsolete as carrier-based aircraft now formed the core of naval power although the US Navy did occasionally utilize the "Iowa" class battleships to supply fire support for land operations in Korea, Vietnam ,and the first Gulf War. Today the gun is still a flexible and effective naval weapon system but only light and medium calibers are utilized, the days of the imposing and powerful heavyweight naval guns having long since passed into a glorious history.

Forts and Castles: To the end of the 19th century

On land, artillery was used not only in battle but also against fixed defenses, in particular city walls and castles. From the start of cities back in the days of the Sumerians, walls had held out invaders. Before the arrival of gunpowder, the stone walls of medieval fortifications could withstand considerable damage from trebuchets and defenders had developed techniques to counter other attacking ploys such as of mining. As long as there was food and water, a garrison could hold out for years. Even with gunpowder, sieges could take a long time—Candia (today's Heraklion) on Crete withstood the Ottoman Turks for twenty years 1648–1668—but that was the exception rather than the rule. Constantinople, capital of an empire that had lasted for 1,500 years, fell to the guns of Mehmed the Conqueror after only fifty-four days.

Soon, the towering, thick curtain walls of castle and city were no protection. Defenses began to be built with cannon in mind: there were more ditches and moats, with earth ramparts to absorb and disperse the energy of cannon fire. Walls exposed to direct fire were vulnerable, so were sunk into ditches fronted by earth slopes. The geometry of these defenses led to star-shaped forts with interlocking lines of fire.

Right: *This aerial view of Totnes Castle from the south shows to advantage the classic motte and bailey layout with the fine circular stone keep on a high mound and the enclosed bailey in front of it. This was the way the Normans held land, with a lord in his castle. Originally a wooden palisade atop a hill (often man-made), by the 14th century these had become stone built. Sieges could last for months and might involve mining to undermine a wall or the use of siege engines, such as trebuchets to hurl rocks and weaken stone walls.*

The star defenses themselves were soon found out by changing technology. Explosive shells rendered them less effective and led to a further evolution. The forts of the 19th and early 20th century were mainly underground structures with few external walkways, difficult to bombard. Surprisingly, the main defenses of these structures—the guns—were in the open, often with only a parapet as protection. Some thought was given to the crew with innovations such disappearing mounts, but in the main it was felt the guns were less likely to be hit in the open than trapped in debris were they casemated (a view, interestingly, that was also arrived at by the Nazi inspector of western fortifications, Generalleutnant Rudolf Schmetzer, in his report on the effects of the D-Day bombardment on the casemated weapons of the Atlantic Wall).

All that changed in the years after World War I. The development of heavy artillery and the trench warfare led to lines of static defense—the Maginot in France being the best-known—where heavily armored forts were emplaced to conduct the defense. Later, in World War II, the Atlantic Wall took these static defenses a stage further. Prickling with long-range guns, coastal, railway, and army batteries, from Spain to the Arctic, the Germans studded the coasts with reinforced concrete structures. On D-Day they lasted less than twenty-four hours.

Since World War II, bombs, missiles, and nuclear weapons seem to have all but rendered forts and fortifications superfluous. Drones and cruise missiles can strike at long range with little or no danger to the operators ... but the rise of asymmetric warfare and terrorism have led to a strange revival. Outside a major war, today it's IEDs and pipe bombs, mortars and "barrack busters" or suicide bombers that are most likely to take a serviceman's life, and today's military bases have once again begun to take on defensive structures.

Left: *Corfe Castle was built by William the Conqueror. In the Civil War it was twice besieged by Parliamentarian forces. The first siege, in 1643, was unsuccessful. Some eighty defenders held the castle for six weeks until relieved. The second siege, of forty-eight days in 1645–1646, ended in treachery and one of the last remaining royalist strongholds in southern England, fell. It had withstood cannon bombardment but could not escape destruction: it was "slighted" on Parliament's orders, a job that took several months and much gunpowder.*

Left: *The castle of Biar has Islamic roots. It was built during the second-half of the 800-year period of Moorish rule when they began to adopt features they had seen in Christian castles. What we know as keeps (in Spain they are called towers of homage) began to appear. The photograph also shows outer curtain, gateway and corner towers which are post-Islamic period replacements. Like the great Crusader castles of the Middle East, the main defensive features start with location, building techniques, and the sheer size of the walls and towers.*

Below Left: *The 16th century saw a major change to castle construction. This is Deal Castle, a coastal artillery fort constructed by Henry VIII between 1539 and 1540. Its purpose was to protect against invasion from France and the Holy Roman Empire. The moated stone castle had sixty-six firing positions for artillery. It was connected to Sandown and Walmer by earthwork defenses.*

Right: *The ruins of Berry Pomeroy castle. On the left side can be seen the original gatehouse and parts of the curtain wall. In the foreground are the substantial remains of the three-story mansion built by Edward Seymour after 1560. In an imposing position atop a hill, the original castle was built at a time of lawlessness during the Wars of the Roses and was intended to be a defendable structure. By the 16th century these troubles had dissipated and Seymour's connection to the crown ensured he had money enough to start the transformation of the castle into a Renaissance great house. We won't know how it would have performed if besieged in the Civil War because it was never garrisoned or attacked.*

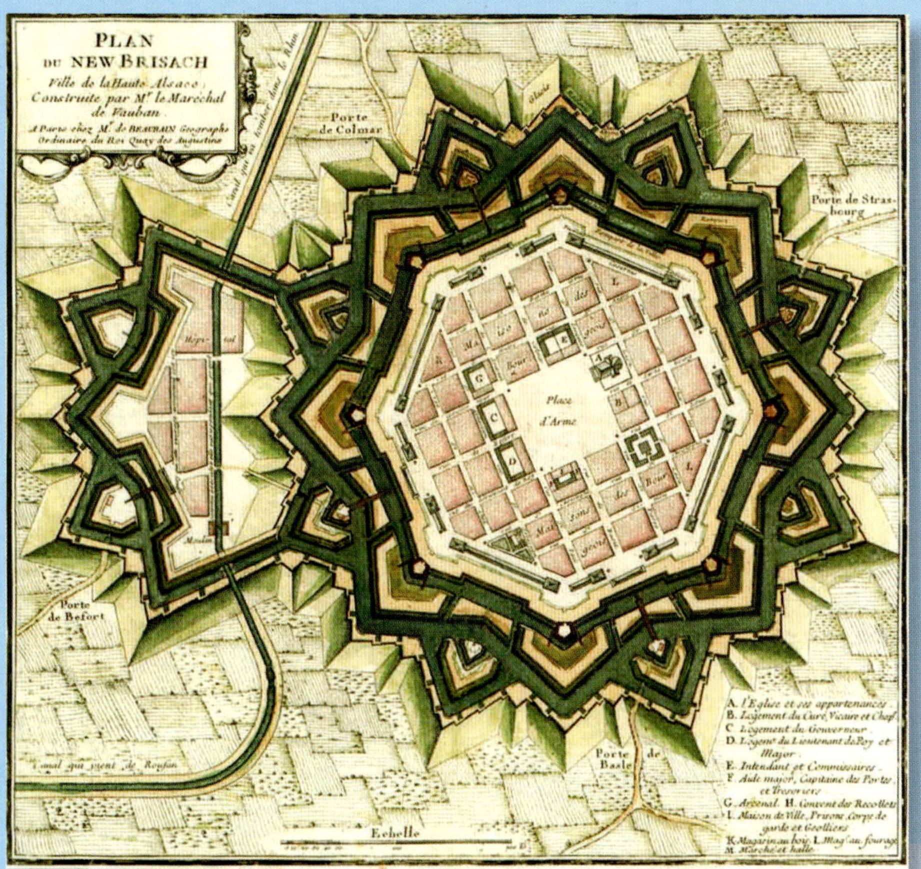

Above Left and Above Right: *Vauban's plan for the town of Neuf-Brisach (***Above Left***) and for a bastioned fort show the 17th century approach to defense.*

Left: *Following the Great Siege of Malta by the Turks in 1565, the Knights Hospitaller improved the defenses in more modern style.*

The photographs on this spread show the way that defenses changed between medieval times and the 17/18th centuries. Gone were high curtain walls and towers which were easy targets for big guns. In their place were lower ramparts with carefully sited firing points over ditches or water obstacles. The great name of the period was Louis XIV's Marquis de Vauban (1633–1707) who fortified 300 cities including Maubeuge (**Right**)*. These are the city's defenses: more important were the ring of forts that surrounded it. They were attacked one by one by the Germans in 1914. Using 305mm and 420mm guns they reduced the forts until Maubeuge was forced to surrender after fifteen days. But while the city fell, it had held 60,000 German soldiers away from the crucial battle of the Marne, which saved Paris and, possibly, France.*

Below Left: *Nothe Fort was built in the second half of the 19th century as part of the major scheme to improve the defenses of Britain's naval bases—in this case Portland, Dorset. Construction began in 1860 and its guns were mounted in 1872. This overhead view shows the distinctive D-shaped layout of the fort but hides the labyrinth of underground passageways. The circular emplacements on the ramparts were for the 6-inch BL guns first mounted in 1902.*

Right: *Fort Delaware on Pea Patch Island in the Delaware River was built for harbor defense but gained most fame for its use as a Civil War prison. Originally conceived as the location for a defensive structure in the late 1790s, the first fort was hastened by the War of 1812 and built in the 1820s. It was completely rebuilt between 1848 and 1860, when it was the largest third-system fortification completed in the United States. During the late 1890s a concrete three-gun battery was added on under the Endicott program.*

Below: *On Portland itself the Verne Citadel was built between 1857–1881. Note the use of the terrain—specifically there are cliffs into the sea (the east side) which formed a natural defensive feature continuing round to the north. On the south side can be seen the deep ditch excavated and surmounted by high earth ramparts to make a formidable defensive feature. Today it's a prison and the detention center has its own protective wall but designed to keep people in rather than prevent entrance!*

Chapter 1: From the Ancient World to the Age of the Cannon

Below Right: *This bronze cannon has an inscription dated the 3rd year of the Zhiyuan era (1332). It was discovered at the Yunju Temple, Fangshan, Beijing.*

Opposite, Left: *A Chinese smoothbore cannon cast in 1675 located inside the former gunpowder factory of Lei Yue Mun Fort. The fort now forms a large part of the Hong Kong Museum of Coastal Defence.*

Opposite, Right: *A granite cannonball.*

Although precise dates are not forthcoming, archeological evidence supports the theory that the Chinese first discovered gunpowder some time in the 9th century during the Tang Dynasty. The first use of artillery using gunpowder occurred some time during the 11th century and the Song's wars against their rivals the Jin, with both sides using gunpowder weapons including increasingly powerful rockets, artillery, and grenades, beginning a process that was to spread west. The Mongols, the Ming, the Muslims, and the Mughals were all consecutively beguiled by the possibilities of these explosive new weapons, though for a period they did little more than scare the horses. The Mongols were especially adept at utilizing them and went on to conquer all the Chinese states. Their early adoption and the success of their armies in both the east and west certainly accelerated the spread of these new gunpowder weapons.

When guns reached Europe there was a further leap in their development. Perhaps the conditions were perfect for an arms race—countless small city states and kingdoms competing against each other ferociously, with a high standard of metallurgical skill that had been developed and handed down through the creation of guilds and masters

passing their knowledge on to apprentices. The new guns were cast like bells or made like barrels with metal staves and reinforcing hoops, and renowned metal-working areas became famous for their gunsmiths too. These gun makers were also often itinerant—for they had to seek out those with the resources and the power to commission such large expensive metal objects.

Older medieval siege engines such as the catapult, the ballista, and the trebuchet were still in use for a considerable time after the invention of gunpowder weapons, but gradually, as the accuracy and dependability of the new armaments increased, so too did their use. Artillery of various sizes was created—guns, having long barrels and a relatively flat trajectory; howitzers, having a short barrel and low-angled trajectory; and mortars, which had the shortest barrels and the highest-angled trajectory. All were muzzle-loaders. With castles and cities surrounded by thick defensive walls the assaulting guns were required to become heavier and heavier. This led to the creation of some spectacular superguns known as bombards, guns that were pushing the boundaries of medieval gunnery to the limit. A bombard mostly fell into the mortar category of the new artillery and they were made as castle killers, to batter down walls.

The main problem with the early cannon was the variation of hand-made ammunition. Each ball had to be carved out of solid stone and so was difficult to size correctly. The solution to the problem was to give the weapon a slightly conical bore, narrowing towards the breech at the rear and widening toward the muzzle at the front, so that balls of different sizes would fit. The problem with widening the bore was that it allowed more of the expanding gas from the ignited black powder to escape as

Below: *A mural at Moldovița Monastery, Romania purports to show the 626 AD siege of Constantinople by the Avars, but the use of cannon is reference to the Ottoman's siege of 1453.*

Opposite, Above: *The siege of Orléans in 1428 was lifted by the arrival of Jeanne d'Arc.*

Opposite, Below: *Charles VIII's troops and artillery enter Naples in 1495. From* Les guerres d'Italie *by Jean-Louis Fournel.*

it propelled the ball forward, reducing the power behind the projectile, but this was compensated for by building ever larger and more powerful bombards.

By the time the Ottoman Turks under Sultan Mehmet II came to the world-famous walls of Constantinople in 1453, bombards had been developed by various cities and states within Europe for some fifty years, but he was the right man in the right place at the right time. This was a sultan with a passion for artillery and a full understanding of the potentially critical role it could play in sieges, for he understood that when used together in batteries they were at their most effective. Possessing more wealth and resources than any other state at that time, Mehmet commissioned the building of the biggest guns he could, using his own weapon manufactories but also searching out other well-known gunsmiths. One such was Orban of Brasov (now in Hungary), who was trying to find a ruler to subsidize the construction of his supergun. Being a European Christian, Orban had first offered his services to the Byzantine ruler Constantine XI, who, though interested, did not have the wherewithal to actually realize the project. Mehmet did and Orban seized his chance—a foundry was built at Adrianople (modern Edirne), where he oversaw the manufacture of both wrought-iron and cast-bronze cannon, including his iron supergun *Viper*, weighing almost twenty tons. This beast required a colossal effort to then be hauled into position—with its own road built and innumerable teams of men and oxen to transport it to the walls of Constantinople, where it joined other giant bombards and cannon, positioned in batteries at the weakest points in the city's fortifications. On April 12, 1453, the world's first concerted big gun artillery barrage exploded into life—and accounts of the time convey the shock and awe experienced in the face of such a sustained bombardment. Although the rate of fire of the biggest bombards was very slow, the range of different artillery pieces used ensured a continuity of intensity and duration that had a tremendous psychological effect on the defenders, for nothing like this had been experienced before. In the end the city fell and a precedent was set. Thereafter the Ottomans continued to build massive superguns which were soon to be seen in Europe as a liability. The fall of Byzantium had set all the Muslim conquerors of the East on the road to impressively large bombards, though with a gradual shift in emphasis as time went on towards the political and technological theater that attended possession of these enormous weapons.

In Europe, however, thinking had changed. The logistical demands of their huge size and weight, combined with transport and ammunition problems, made big guns almost worthless. Giant bombards often blew themselves (and their human crews) apart, as they were often made and operated at the front edge of weapon development, using materials and techniques which often fell short through inherent weaknesses in construction. Poor metallurgy resulted in fragilities in the barrel or breech such as trapped air pockets and undetected fault-line fractures. Guns were also tested and "proven" by being fired beyond their tolerance in a misconceived idea of consolidating them before use. The immense pressures generated by firing necessitated the biggest guns to be cooled for hours before being fired again. Cumulative use weakened the guns and made them dangerously prone to rupturing or exploding without warning. Besides the metal, the proportions in the mixing of the gunpowder propellant and the amount used in each firing were also critical and any mistakes would lead to disaster, often resulting in a barrel explosion.

For all their impressive size the biggest bombards were only partially successful and their effectiveness on the battlefield was disproportionate to their huge logistical demands and financial costs. The trade off was in the fear they stirred in the enemy. In reality the resources used in their construction could instead be used to produce several guns of a smaller caliber that could still achieve the same effect by being used concentrated together in a battery. Being lighter and less bulky, these guns were also much easier to transport and deploy and their ammunition became more potent with the introduction of the cast-iron cannonball, which could be standardized in production and were much more devastating that their stone predecessors.

Thus in the second half of the 15th century, the development in siege technology moved on and other than as impressive gate guards on display outside palaces or in market squares, the largest bombards began to disappear from the leading artillery arsenals of Europe. But the idea of a supergun hadn't died.

Right: *Artillery was not widely employed in Central Asia prior to the 16th century, even though Chinese mortars had been known to the Mongols for many years. In 1526, the First Battle of Panipat saw the introduction of massed artillery tactics to Indian warfare. The battle is shown in an illustration from the Baburnama.*

Far Right: *By the time of Akbar the Great (1542–1605), cannon played a key role in Indian warfare as shown by the fall of Ranthambore Fort, the most powerful fortress in India. This image from the Baburnama is of bullocks dragging siege-guns up hill during his attack on the fort, 1568.*

Opposite: *The Jaivan Cannon at Jaigarh Fort, Jaipur, India was cast in 1720 by Jai Singh II, a formidable ruler in Northern India whose strength lay in the large number of artillery pieces and copious munitions. Four elephants were used to swivel it around on its axis.*

Naval Weapons

Cannons firing a shot heavy enough to damage an enemy vessel began to be fitted aboard ships in the 15th century. Surprisingly, many of these early cannon were breech-loading, partly because of the lack of space and tackle available to load a gun through its muzzle. The charge and projectile were carried in an iron cylinder which was wedged behind the fixed barrel. However, these were usually a poor fit which only worsened with usage. These early cannon had barrels made up of strips of wrought iron held together by iron hoops and sealed with molten lead. A later development saw barrels constructed of short lengths of iron tubes with flanged ends (similar to a cotton reel) held together by wrought iron bars wrapped around the flanges. Both these types lay in a trough cut out of a heavy timber block which resulted in very little provision for adjustment of aim.

By the mid-16th century foundries had perfected methods of producing cast-iron cannon which could be mounted on wheeled frames. At that time King Henry VIII's great ships

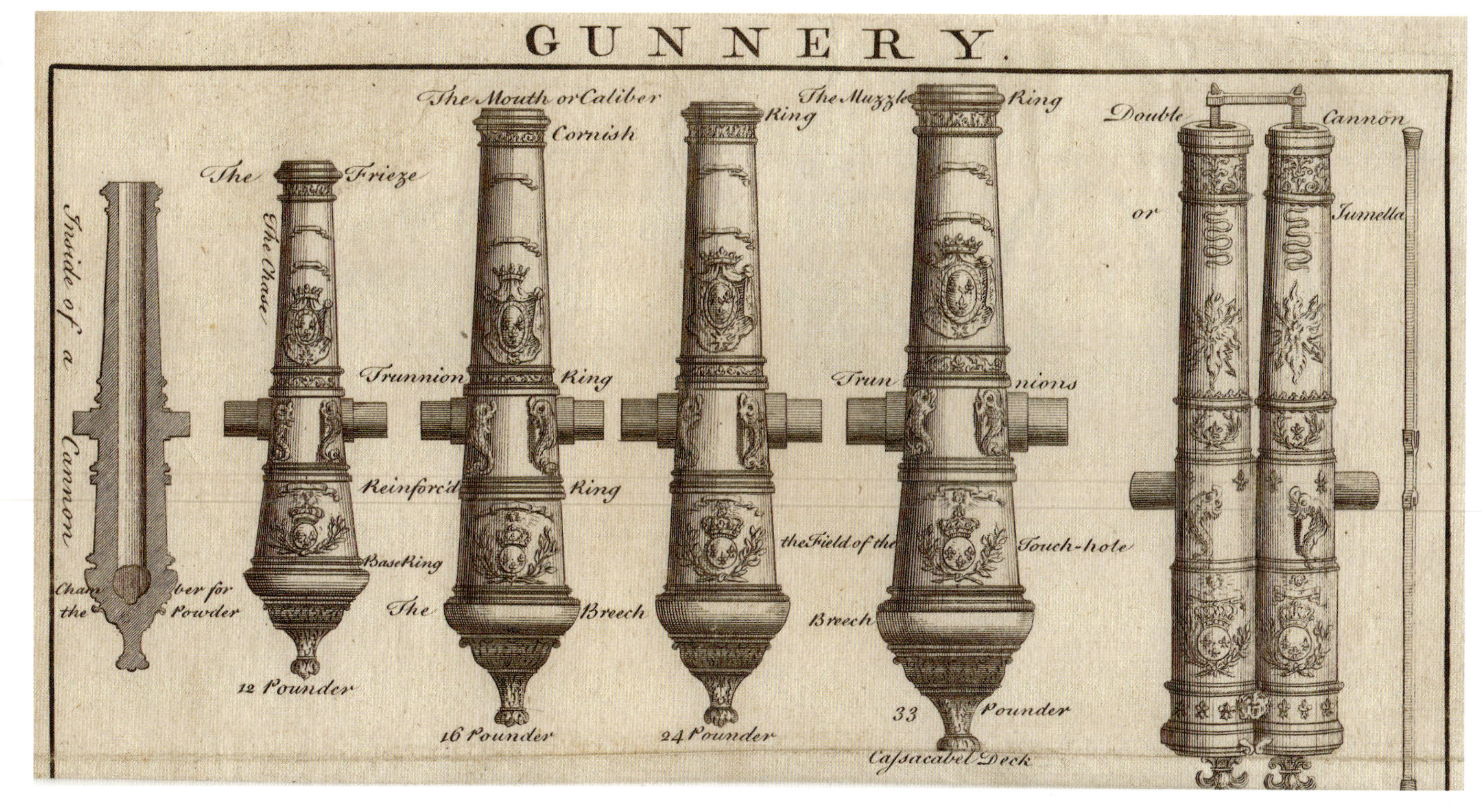

Right: *A 17th century illustration showing the relative size of various cannon types.*

Opposite: *A list of cannon types taken from a 17th century treatise on naval gunnery. In each case the range is given in paces (generally accepted as around 30 inches), the left-hand column relating to when the gun is fired horizontally and the other to when the gun is tilted at maximum practical elevation.*

	Paces. Level.	Paces. Utmoſt Random.
A *Baſe* ſhoots ——	60	600
A *Rabinet*, ——	70	700
A *Falconet*, ——	90	900
A *Falcon*, ——	130	1300
Minion ordinary ——	120	1200
Minion largeſt, ——	125	1250
Sacker leaſt, ——	150	1500
Sacker ordinary, ——	160	1600
Sacker old Sort, ——	163	1630
Demi-culverine leaſt,	174	1740
Demi-culverine ordinary	175	1750
Demi-culverine old Sort	178	1780
Culverine leaſt, ——	180	1800
Culverine ordinary,	181	1810
Culverine largeſt,	183	1830
Demi-cannon leaſt,	156	1560
Demi cannon ordinary,	162	1620
Demi-cannon large,	180	1800
Cannon-Royal ——	185	1850

carried two decks of heavy guns, the larger pieces— muzzle-loaders—on the lower deck while lighter pieces, a mixture of breech and muzzle-loaders, were on the upper deck. By the time of the Spanish Armada in 1588 the breech-loaders had mostly disappeared, but there was no standardization in the type of gun carried. A single ship might carry as many as seven or eight varieties all bearing exotic sounding names such as Culverin, Saker, Minion, and Falcon. The weight of shot varied from half a pound in a Rabinet to 60lb in a Cannon (or Cannon Royale).

In the 17th century some standardization of ships and their guns was introduced, and from then until the mid-19th century there was little change except for a gradual increase in the size of individual ships. The largest gun mounted was the 42-pdr, but over time this was phased out and most first rate ships carried 32-pdrs on the lower deck and a mix of 24-pdrs and 18-pdrs on the middle and upper decks. In the latter half of the 18th century the Royal Navy, and other navies subsequently, adopted a lighter weapon known as a "carronade." Intended for short-range engagements it utilized a much smaller powder charge which, in turn, allowed for a lighter and shorter barrel such that, for example, a 32-pdr carronade was a quarter the weight of a standard 32-pdr.

After the Napoleonic wars the Royal Navy standardized on the 32-pdr for its major warships but in 1837 it adopted shell-firing guns following the lead of the French Navy. These were produced by boring out existing 32-pdrs to 8-inch or 10-inch caliber and at the same time a new 68-pdr weapon was introduced. These were all muzzle-loaders but the first British ironclad battleship HMS *Warrior* (1861) was also reintroduced breech-loading guns in the form of Armstrong 7-inch 110-pdr. However these were not successful and muzzle-loaders reigned supreme for another 20 years.

1400–1430: *Faule Magd* Bombard

Faule Magd (Lazy Maid) was a bombard made of wrought iron in Saxony some time between 1410 and 1430. With a cannonball weight of 106lb, she was originally fired from the ground or a cradle but was mounted on a mobile gun carriage of oak in 1600.

Faule Magd now resides in the excellent Bundeswehr Militärhistorisches Museum in Dresden, Germany.

FAULE MAGD

15th Century
Saxony
Maker: Unknown
Location: Bundeswehr Military History Museum, Dresden, Germany

Barrel length: 7ft 8in
Weight: 1.5 tons
Caliber: 345mm (13.6 inches)
Max range: Unknown

15th-century: *Pumhart von Steyr* Bombard

Pumhart von Steyr is the largest-known wrought-iron medieval bombard by caliber ever made—only the bronze cast Tsar Cannon has a larger caliber. It was made some time in the early 15th century in Liezen, Styria in Austria, commissioned by the Hapsburg dynasty of the Austro-Hungarian Empire—an area known for its ironworking heritage.

It could fire a 2.625ft-diameter stone ball shot weighing almost 1,545lb (*Faule Magd* fired a shot of 106lb; *Faule Mette* between 700 and 950lb) to a range of around 1,970ft. Built as castle-killing supergun, with all its attendant problems of transport and rate of fire, it too must have been made following the mindset of the age—as a political and technological statement.

PUMHART VON STEYR

15th century
Austria
Maker: Unknown
Location: Army History Museum, Vienna, Austria

Overall length: 8ft 6in
Barrel length: 4ft 8in
Weight: 8 tons
Caliber: 800mm (31.5 inches)
Max range: Unknown

Right: *Today the* Pumhart von Steyr *is on display in one of the artillery halls of the Heeresgeschichtliches Museum at Vienna.*

Opposite: Faule Magd *was only latterly mounted on a carriage. At first it would have been fired from the ground or a cradle.*

1409: *Faule Grete* Bombard

FAULE GRETE

15th Century
Teutonic Knights
Maker: Heynrich Dumechen
Location: None extant

Overall length: 8ft 2.5in
Barrel length: 4ft 11in
Weight: 4.6 tons
Caliber: 500mm
(19.7 inches)
Max range: 657yd

Made in 1409 from cast bronze by the gunmaker Heynrich Dumechen in the Teutonic Knights' capital city of Marienburg, *Faule Grete* (Lazy Grete) could fire stone ball ammunition up to 375lb (170kg). The knights were well-versed in the manufacture of bombards and employed them in their defeat at Grunwald in 1410.

Faule Grete proved her worth when she was borrowed by Frederick I of Brandenburg, who used it to reduce all opposition amongst knights in his own state as he set about laying the foundations of the Hohenzollern dynasty. There exist only a few engravings of this mortar-like bombard and its ultimate fate is unknown.

Below: *A wrought iron bombard of similar size to* Faule Grete *cast in 1450. It could launch a 285lb stone ball, range around 1,500ft.*

Opposite, Right: *A modern reconstruction of the 1414 bombardment of Friesack castle with the* Faule Grete.

Left: *This bombard—*La Fère*— was made from wrought iron during the second half of the 15th century. Wrought-iron bars were welded together and bound with circular reinforcing bracelets in a process known as* "à tonoille."

1411: *Faule Mette* Bombard

FAULE METTE

15th Century
City of Brunswick, Holy Roman Empire
Maker: Henning Bussenschutte
Location: None extant

Overall length: 10ft
Weight: 8.5 tons
Caliber: 800mm (31.5 inches)
Max range: 1.5 miles

Cast in bronze in 1411 in the German city of Brunswick by the gunmaker Henning Bussenschutte, *Faule Mette* (Lazy Mette) was another early big gun. Its "Faule" prefix, "Lazy," referred to its slow rate of transportation and fire but could just as easily refer to its history as well, for although it was fired a dozen times it was never used militarily, but rather to enhance the prestige of the city geopolitically.

Faule Mette certainly impressed those who saw her and her fame spread. *In Memoirs of the House of Brunswick,* author Henry Rimius talks of how the "European nations were taught to give, as it were, Wings to Lead and Iron, and to multiply the Instruments of Slaughter and Destruction." The House of Brunswick increased its range of "Guns and Pieces of Ordinance ... besides those of common size caused an extraordinary one to be cast ... called the *Faule Mette*." She could fire stone ball shot weighing between 710lb and 933lb using a gunpowder load ranging from 53lb to 73lb with a range of 8,012ft.

For over 300 years *Faule Mette* stood ceremonial guard in the City of Brunswick until in 1717 she was melted down in another hour of need and recast into several lighter field pieces that were infinitely more practical.

Right and Far Right: *Two contemporary illustrations of* Faule Mette.

Left: *The later years of the 14th century showed significant improvements in the manufacture of firearms and increasing numbers were used on battlefields. Venice used them effectively against Genoa in the War of Chioggia where gunpowder artillery was used from ships. During the Hussite wars, the Hussites employed firearms extensively from armored carts (*Wagenburg*) enabling them to defeat German knights. Firearms also were used in the final battles of the Hundred Years' War. This bombard-mortar was founded on the orders of Pierre d'Aubusson of the Knights of Saint John of Jerusalem to Rhodes. In 1480 the knights had withstood a siege and knew that the Ottomans would be back. (They were right. The city fell after a hard siege in 1522.) Today, it's in the Musée de l'Armée in Paris, and is identified as the largest known bombard in history.*

1440s: *Dulle Griet* Bombard

Like her younger older sister *Mons Meg*, *Dulle Griet* (Mad Meg) was made for Duke Philip the Good of Burgundy by the Walloon gunmaker Jehan Cambier. The two superguns were constructed in exactly the same fashion with wrought-iron longitudinal bars reinforced with iron hoops mounted while red-hot then quickly water-cooled to shrink fit. *Mad Meg* is larger and heavier than *Mons Meg*, weighing 12.5 tons and could fire round stone shot weighing 550lb to a distance of 2,734 yards or a 770lb iron shot about half the distance. The exact date of *Dulle Griet*'s construction is not known, but she preceded her sister. In 1452 she was used by the city of Ghent against a rival city, Oudenarde. In the course of the battle, *Mad Meg* was captured and only returned in 1578. She can be seen today, painted red as she was originally, near the Friday Market square in the old town.

DULLE GRIET

15th Century
City of Ghent, Holy Roman Empire
Maker: Jehan Cambier
Location: Ghent, Belgium

Overall length: 17ft 2in
Barrel length: 11ft 4in
Weight: 12.5 tons
Caliber: 640mm (25.2 inches)
Max range: 1.6 miles

Opposite: *Commonly known as the "Big Red Devil"* Dulle Griet *sits in Groot Kanonplein, next to the River Leie.*

Left: *A figure from Flemish folklore, Pieter Breughel the Elder painted* Dulle Griet *as a virago, leading an army of women to pillage Hell.*

MONS MEG

15th Century
Burgundian
Maker: Jehan Cambier
Location: Edinburgh Castle

Overall length: 15 feet
Barrel length: 9ft 2in
Weight: 7.7 tons
Caliber: 510mm (20 inches)
Max range: 1.9 miles

1449: *Mons Meg* Bombard

The medieval bombard *Mons Meg* was commissioned by Duke Philip the Good of Burgundy from the Walloon gunmaker Jehan Cambier and given as a wedding present to King James II of Scotland, who in 1449 married the Duke's great niece, Mary of Gueldres, to support him in his war against their mutual enemy, the English. *Mons Meg* is a smaller version of a previous commission from the duke (*Dulle Griet*) and made by the same man.

The gun has two distinct parts, the powder chamber and the barrel, both being reinforced with iron hoops and fused into one mass. The powder chamber is built to take the force of the propellant explosion and is made from small pieces of iron hammer-welded together to make a single solid wrought iron forging. The barrel cylinder (or "chase") is made of longitudinal strips of wrought iron arranged like the staves of a barrel and hammer-welded together. It is attached to grooves in the powder chamber using lugs, and then both elements were reinforced with iron hoops driven tightly over them while hot, then cooled swiftly to shrink and tighten them. An internal conical shape of the gun barrel enabled the fitting of imprecise handmade ammunition.

Mons Meg was capable of blasting 330–397lb gunstones up to two miles. Both sandstone and granite shot were used and black powder was the propellant charge, although there is no specific data about the amount required. The bombard was tested successfully in 1449, and given by the Duke to James II in 1454. Her first unsubstantiated use was at the siege of Roxburgh Castle in 1460, where James II is recorded as having used cannon and was in fact killed by one misfiring and exploding, though not *Mons Meg*.

James IV returned *Mons Meg* to action in 1489 with his attacks on Dumbarton castle, using her in the second, successful, siege. In 1513 he invaded England again, laying siege to Norham Castle. His guns, including *Mons Meg*, pounded the outer defenses for several days until the walls were breached and the outer ward taken, with the castle surrendering soon after.

Mons Meg's enormous weight and the difficulties of transportation made her use problematical and although maintained as an active weapon, after James's foray she was confined to Edinburgh Castle and used only on ceremonial occasions. In 1558 she was fired to celebrate the marriage of Mary Queen of Scots to the French Dauphin. However when fired in 1681 to celebrate the birthday of the Duke of Albany (later King James VII) her barrel burst and she was then left abandoned for many years.

In 1754 following the Jacobite rebellion *Meg* was taken as a precaution to London. In 1829, after 75 years in England a popular appeal (in which Sir Walter Scott was prominent) culminated in a request to King George IV, and *Mons Meg* was restored to Scotland. She made a triumphant return to her home castle, Edinburgh, escorted by cavalry and infantry from the docks at Leith. She is still there.

Above Left: Mons Meg *is in the collection of the Royal Armouries, but on loan to Historic Scotland and located at Edinburgh Castle.*

Left: Mons Meg, *the six-ton 15th-century cannon that guards the parapets of Edinburgh Castle.*

Above: *Closeup of the burst barrel of* Mons Meg.

1464: The Great Turkish Bombard

THE GREAT TURKISH BOMBARD

15th Century
Turkey
Maker: Munir Ali
Location: Fort Nelson, Portsmouth, England

Overall length: 17ft 2in
Barrel length: 7ft 8in
Weight: 18.5 tons
Caliber: 630mm (24.8 inches)
Max range: 1 mile +

Sultan Mehmet II learned much from his successful siege of Constantinople in 1453 and had a lifelong interest in the art of war and its technology, especially state of the art weaponry such as artillery. In 1464 he commissioned another supergun to be built by his engineer Munir Ali.

Cast in bronze with a weight of eighteen tons, an overall length of 17ft 2in, the separate powder chamber and the barrel connect by way of a screw mechanism, allowing the gun to be more easily transported in two separate pieces, the breech end of the cannon being shorter and of a slightly smaller diameter than the barrel, ensuring a conical internal tapering to fit the inevitable variation in handmade ammunition. Both parts are cast with prominent double moldings at either end which are joined using sixteen crosspieces that fit into sockets for the levers used in the joining of both sections together. They are also divided by rounded moldings, five on the chase and three on the breech. Despite this innovation, the Great Turkish Bombard required a road building crew ahead of it and a huge carrying team to move this massive and cumbersome weapons system. When being fired, the gun was mounted on wooden beds with another large wooden recoil bed behind it and it was capable of firing over a mile.

Along with other ancient Ottoman superguns and cannon, the Great Turkish Bombard saw action more than 340 years later in 1807, when a British Royal Navy force sailed up the Dardanelles Straits to bombard Istanbul during the Anglo-Turkish War of 1807–1809. These ancient guns were loaded with powder and various kinds of munitions that were then fired at the British ships, with 42 killed and 235 wounded by the end of the engagement.

Impressed with its size and age, over the course of the next few decades, various attempts were made by the British to buy or hustle the Great Bombard from the Turks. Finally in 1866, on the occasion of a state visit, Sultan Abdülaziz gave it to Queen Victoria as gift. It then became part of the Royal Armories collection, being put on display at the Tower of London before eventually being moved to Fort Nelson, overlooking Portsmouth Harbor in Hampshire, where it resides to this day.

Right: *Muzzle view of the Great Turkish Bombard at Fort Nelson, Hampshire, England. The bombard was also known as Şahi Topu or The Dardanelles Gub.*

1524: *Kanone Greif* Kartouwe

KANONE GREIF

16th century
Trier
Maker: Simon of Frankfurt
Location: Ehrenbreitstein Fortress, Koblenz, Germany

Overall length: 16ft 6in
Weight: 9 tons +
Caliber: 280mm (11 inches)
Range: Unknown

In 1524 the Trier Elector, Archbishop Richard von Greiffenklau zu Vollrads, commissioned a gunmaker named Simon from Frankfurt to make a kartouwe—the Kanone Greif or *Griffin*. Cast in bronze and weighing over nine tons, the *Griffin* could fire stone balls of up to 177lb, using at least 88lb of black powder. It was kept at the Ehrenbreitstein fortress in Koblenz, and swapped hands several times between the Germans and the French during various wars between the two countries. In 1799 it was relocated by the French to Metz, but when that city was besieged they removed it to Paris. In 1940, following the fall of Paris, it was repossessed by the Germans, only to be taken once again by the French following Germany's defeat. Finally, in 1984 as an act of goodwill and reconciliation the French returned the *Griffin* to its rightful owners and it now rests in the Landesmuseum in its home city of Koblenz once more. Despite gunpowder traces in the barrel confirming that it has been fired at some time, again as seems a common fate of these largest of guns, there is no historical record of the *Griffin*'s use in war.

Left: *There's an inscription on* Griffin*:*

The Griffin *is my name.*
Simon cast me.
I serve my gracious master of Trier.
Where he called me to fight,
there I will split spikes and walls.

Indian 16th Century Cannons

The Gunpowder Empires of Asia—Ottomans, Safavids, and Mughals—spread the use of firearms and cannon in the 15th and 16th centuries. From Constantinople to Delhi significant battles took place with musketeers and artillery at their heart. Varna (1444), Constantinople (1453), Chaldiran (1514), Panipat (1526), Jam (1528), Talikota (1565)—these important battles led to a tradition of gunmaking that continued on into the 17th century. The three big guns illustrated here exemplify this industry in India.

Malik-i-Maidan

Cast in 1549 from bell metal by Muhammad Bin Husain Rumiat Ahmadnagar, the *Malik-i-Maidan* (Master of the Battlefield) gained its name after its success at the battle of Talikota at which the Vijayangar empire was routed. On show at Bijapur Fort in Karnataka, it has a diameter of nearly five feet, weighs fifty-five tons, is 14ft 7in long, and has a muzzle bore of 700mm (28 inches). The muzzle is decorated in the form of a lion's head with carved open jaws and an elephant between the jaws.

Rajagopala

This forge-welded iron cannon was created at Kollumedu near Thanjavur in 1620 during the reign of Raghunatha Nayak (1600–1645) with help from Danish metallurgists. There are forty-three long iron plates bound by ninety-four iron rings. Positioned to protect Thanjavur from enemy attack through Keelavasal (the East Gate), it can still be seen in the Tamil Nadu city. It is a foot in diameter, twenty-six feet long, weighs twenty-four tons, and has a muzzle of 150mm (six inches).

Dal Madal

Maharaja Bir Hambir, the forty-ninth king of the Mallabhum, ruled 1565–1620 and commissioned this famous cannon. Built by Jagannath Karmakar, in Bengali *Dal Madal* means destruction of your enemy. The cannon is twenty-six feet long and weighs 24.25 tons. It is forge-welded using sixty-three iron plates and has a diameter of 285mm. There is a myth that Lord Madanmohan—the local name of Lord Krishna—fired the weapon to protect Bishnupur from attack by Maratha dacoits.

Opposite: *Similar to the* Griffin, *although smaller, this is a Kartouwe in the Army History Museum in Vienna. The Kartouwe were siege guns with a caliber of around 200mm. They were also made as double (closer to* Griffin*), half or quarter Kartouwen.*

Below, from Left to Right

Left: *The* Malik-i-Maidan *at Bijapur Fort.*

Center: Rajagopala *beerangi (cannon) at Thanjavur.*

Right: Dal Madal Kaman *(cannon).*

1585: The Tsar Cannon

TSAR CANON

16th Century
Russia
Maker: Andrei Chokhov
Location: Cannon Court, Moscow, Russia

Overall length: 19ft 6in
Weight: 43 tons
Caliber: 890mm (35 inches)
Range: Unknown
(never fired in anger)

Located on the west side of the Kremlin's largest square, Ivanovskaya, in Moscow and part of its extensive artillery collection sits the awesome Tsar Cannon. With a caliber of 890mm it is the largest bombard cannon in the world. It was cast in bronze in 1585 in Moscow by the renowned cannon-maker Andrei Chokhov on the orders of the Tsar Feodor Ioannovich and is decorated with that prince personified as a horseman in the beautiful decorative friezes that cover the gun—a testament to Russian metallurgical skill. Although the barrel contains traces of having been used, the fact that this supergun has no record of ever having being fired in anger would seem to invalidate it as an authentic weapons system. Technically, by the time it was made it was already virtually obsolete for the 1580s, gigantic bombards having being abandoned in most of Europe by this time.

But bombards have a political as well as a military function, and the Tsar Cannon is preeminently a psychological and political statement. It was built more to be seen rather than used and on view to both the Russian public and foreigners alike in the center of Moscow, the Tsar cannon succeeded in conveying the power of the Kremlin and the Muscovite royal line.

In 1835, the Tsar Cannon was fixed onto a carriage specially cast for it at the Berdt factory in St. Petersburg. This carriage is purely decorative and could neither transport the gun effectively, nor handle the force of it being fired. Four hollow decorative iron cannonballs, which it could never have shot as they were larger than its caliber, were made at the same time. The Tsar cannon harked back to an earlier time of stone-shot ammunition and an old nickname the "Russian Shotgun" implied that it was meant to shoot 1,765lb stone grapeshot rather than solid balls.

Left and Opposite: *The Tsar Cannon would have fired stone shot rather than the balls in front of it.*

Chapter 2: The Development of Artillery

Lt Gen Jean Baptiste Vaquette de Gribeauval introduced a new production system for French cannon during the 18th century, the efficacy of which was highlighted by Napoleon. The canon de 24 Gribeauval (as seen here) saw extensive use during the period.

War spurs weapon development—and the shooting never stops. During the 17th and 18th centuries cannon became commonplace on the battlefield in large numbers. Heavy mortars based on the German design were still used in sieges with their munitions little refined, otherwise as ordnance became more explosive artillery became lighter—in order to be more easily portable on a battlefield still dominated by cavalry and infantry. Increasingly, smaller cannon were used because of their improved rate of fire. For example, Gustavus Adolphus, the Swedish king (1611–1632), didn't use 12-pdr or larger cannon on the battlefield. Mobile mortars, too, were introduced, although it wouldn't be until World War I that the truly man-portable mortar was invented.

This meant more standardization to ease logistical burdens—particularly for ammunition. Production also became more standardized, beginning with the work of a French artillery engineer—Jean-Baptise de Gribeauval—who reformed his army's artillery, which would enable another French artillery officer, Napoleon Bonaparte, to perfect his portable barrage technique of cannon used in fire support batteries before an infantry and cavalry assault.

In the 19th century, the Napoleonic and Crimean wars in Europe and the American Civil War saw major improvements which further increased the potency of artillery. Although the massive old muzzle-loading bombards were still built and used in parts of Asia, Europe's frenetic weapons' development continued to move away from that kind of supergun. From a heavyweight perspective this period up to the beginning of World War I had a slow start, before burgeoning industrial development enabled a return to larger format artillery. Indeed, by 1850 Europe and America's industrial advancement had led to a radical transformation in all aspects of life, making it visibly similar to the modern world of today. Infrastructure, transport, and communication systems, factories and machines of all kinds began to emerge in a flurry of simultaneous experiments and discoveries. These technological advances also enabled the construction of more sophisticated and powerful weapon systems. In gun construction, ammunition, and propellant mix a revolution was taking place.

New construction techniques were employed to produce better quality and bigger weapons. In the United States there was Thomas Jackson Rodman, who cast his cannon around a hollow core, cooled from the inside by running water and so increasing its density and strength. Rodman went on to build some massive seacoast superguns.

Another American, Robert Parker Parrott, patented a new method with his cast and wrought-iron cannon, again using water cooling for the inside of the cast barrel, completed with a wrought-iron strengthening band around the breech. Its success spurred on larger versions.

Technological advances included the continued refinement of rifling the inner barrel. Putting a gyroscopic spin on a fired shell increased its range, stability and accuracy. Although rifling had been invented earlier in the 15th century, it took the more advanced industrial and engineering skills of the 19th century to perfect it and as the necessary engineering ability evolved so rifling began to become the norm.

In Britain in 1852 Armstrong developed a radical new design—a cast and coil-welded, rifled, breech-loading 3-pdr gun which was initially very successful in China and New Zealand when used against less militarily developed armies. However the British Army, with its traditional gunners ill-trained to the new weapon, preferred the old-fashioned approach and so Armstrong went back to muzzle-loaders (RML). His construction methods greatly increased the strength and accuracy of his weapons, and although having his own doubts about the suitability of this system for superlarge versions, he was encouraged to do so by the Government, culminating in the 100-ton gun.

In 1855 another British engineer and designer, Joseph Whitworth, inventor of rifles, guns, bullets and shells, designed a large rifled breech-loading (RBL) gun with a 2.75-inch bore, firing a 12lb 11oz projectile with a range of about six miles. He also designed a spirally grooved cylindroconic

Below: *Battery Rodgers was erected in 1863 overlooking the Potomac River near Jones' Point as part of Washington's defenses. Today its position is marked by a marker: "Here stood Battery Rodgers, built in 1863 to prevent enemy ships from passing up the Potomac River. The battery had a perimeter of 30 yards and mounted five 200 pounder Parrott guns and one 15-inch Rodman. It was deactivated in 1867." This photo of the battery shows the huge 15-inch Rodman (left) and a Parrott 200-pdr.*

Below: *A 32-pdr takes part in the siege of Sebastopol. The artist, Capt M.A. Biddulph RA, served as assistant engineer in the trenches outside the city, helped repulse a Russian sortie on October 26, 1854, and assisted in the three bombardments of the fortress.*

shell. Although the British government ultimately chose the Armstrong weapons, Whitworth's guns and shells saw service in the American Civil War. In 1887 the Armstrong and Whitworth companies merged and the new company became famous worldwide for its weapons and munitions. By then steel had become the new material of choice with which to make heavy guns. In 1856 the German Alfred Krupp began producing a muzzle-loading rifled gun made from a single ingot of solid cast steel. The weapon soon made a name for itself, was adopted by the Prussian army, and began to sell worldwide.

The familiar cone shape of today's shells was another key development in the evolution of artillery. Most of the above-mentioned gun makers also made their own munitions, to fit the specific rifling in their barrels. Some rifled the shell or added guiding lugs or a covering of lead to ensure a more precise fit. Getting a government contract enabled certain guns and shells to become established. In Britain in 1867 Maj. William Palliser introduced his conic armor-piercing shell that was adopted for the larger types of rifled muzzle-loaders at the Woolwich Arsenal. Similar types of explosive and armor-piercing shells were produced by the Germans and the French around the same time. Palliser also invented a retro rifling fitment for smoothbore cannon, which enabled a new lease of life for many obsolescent muzzle-loaders.

Along with cylindroconical shells replacing round shot, the old black powder propellant was surpassed by a group of more powerful explosives that were discovered virtually simultaneously in different parts of Europe. These new smokeless powders did not foul the barrel as the old powder did, enabling a quicker reload time and leading to the eventual development of automatically reloading weapons. In 1846 German chemist Christian Schönbein invented guncotton made from nitrocellulose, which unless kept dry and cool spontaneously ignited. In 1847 Italian Chemist Ascanio Sobrero invented nitroglycerin. In 1865 British chemist Frederick Abel established a safe process for the manufacture of guncotton which kept it stable. Swede Alfred Nobel came up with a detonator in 1863 and a blasting cap in 1865. He followed this up with the invention of dynamite in 1867 and gelignite in 1875. In 1884 French chemist Paul Vieille invented the first practical smokeless gunpowder with Poudre B. In Britain Abel and Dewar came up with cordite

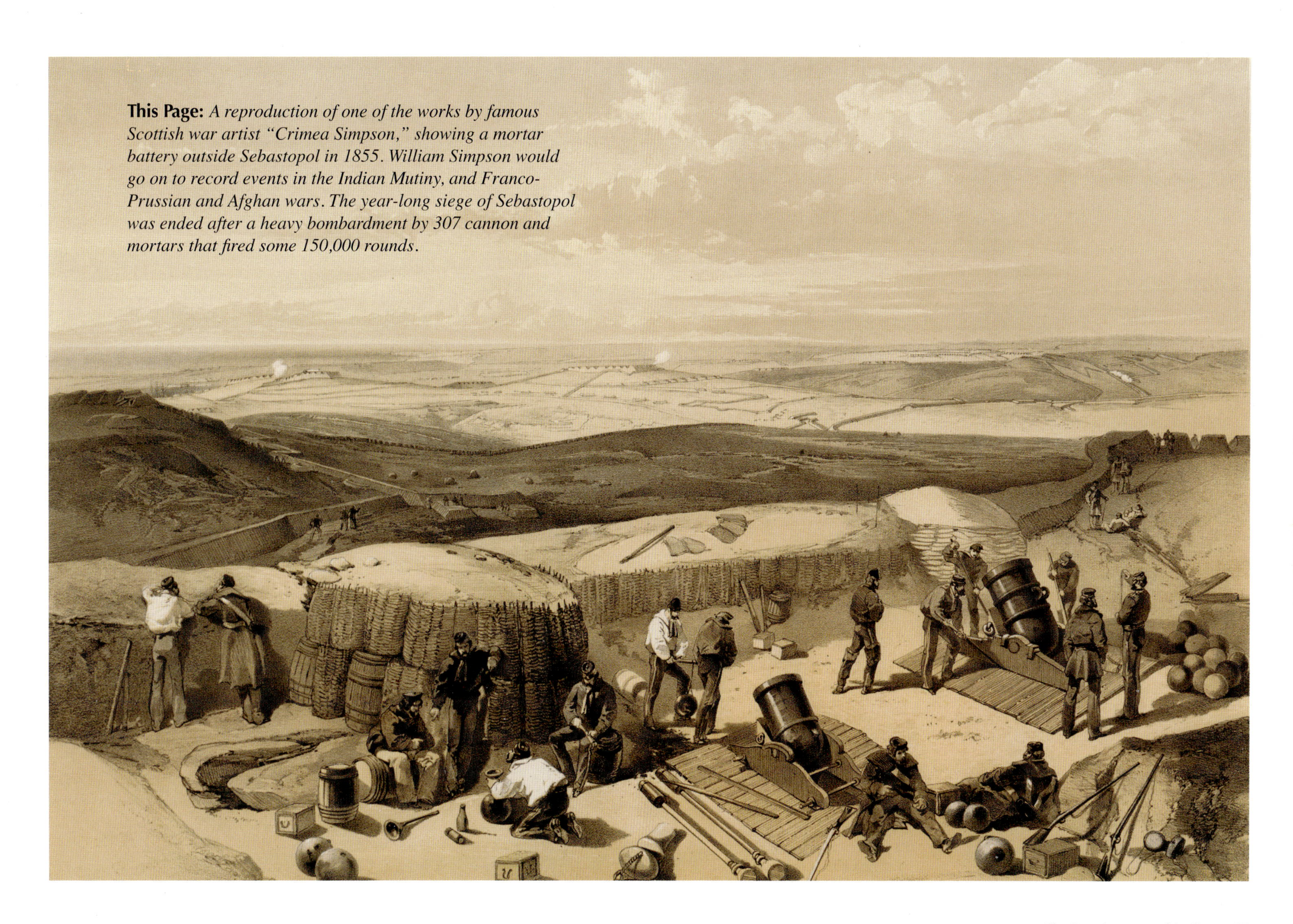

This Page: *A reproduction of one of the works by famous Scottish war artist "Crimea Simpson," showing a mortar battery outside Sebastopol in 1855. William Simpson would go on to record events in the Indian Mutiny, and Franco-Prussian and Afghan wars. The year-long siege of Sebastopol was ended after a heavy bombardment by 307 cannon and mortars that fired some 150,000 rounds.*

in 1889 while in America Rodman and Parrot experimented with new propellants and shells for their guns.

As all these new chemical explosives became available there was a corresponding frenzy of new developments in munitions and weapon systems, and the war at that time to test many of them was underway in America. It is often posited that the American Civil War was the first one of the modern era—with the use of railroad transport systems, telegraph communications, aerial observation and photography as well as the introduction of the machine gun, the repeating rifle, turreted ironclad ships, torpedoes and mines and use of the most powerful heavy artillery.

Even though this revolutionary period continued to use older tried and tested equipment that led back briefly to the final flowering massive muzzle-loaders before breech-loaders became the new norm, the European and American industrial revolutions and their modern production methods laid the ground for a new era of artillery manufacture. The switch from cast iron and bronze to steel, the refinement of rifling, standardization, cylindroconical explosive shells, new more powerful propellants and the development of indirect fire support tactics led directly to today's modern weapons.

Europe was now locked in a competition for the spoils of industrialized war—colonies and the resources of other countries who were technologically less advanced and therefore ripe for exploitation. This increasingly competitive arms race was heading inexorably to a confrontation of a size and kind never witnessed before, using industrial processes to systematize warfare on an unparalleled scale. The scene was set for the first truly global war.

Naval Weapons

At the start of the 19th century almost all warships were armed with cast iron smoothbore muzzle-loading cannon firing solid round shot and any decisive engagement was fought at very close range. One hundred years later they carried steel breech-loading guns with rifled barrels capable of accurately firing a variety of specialized munitions including armor-piercing and high-explosive shells over ranges in excess of 10,000 yards. Of course such a transformation did not happen overnight: developments generally followed the pattern of land based artillery as already described. However considerable thought and effort was devoted to finding the optimum methods of mounting and operating heavy guns aboard a ship. When HMS *Warrior*, the world's first iron-hulled armored warship, commissioned in 1861 her mix of 68-pdr ML and Armstrong 110-pdr RBL guns were arranged in the traditional broadside configuration. In 1862, during the Civil War, the Confederate broadside ironclad CSS *Virginia*, mounting ten heavy guns, engaged the Federal USS *Monitor* armed with only two 11-inch Dahlgren guns, but these were mounted in a revolutionary steam-operated armored turret. Although the outcome of the battle was indeterminate, its effect on the design and arming of future warships was profound in demonstrating the value of armor and the flexibility of the rotating turret.

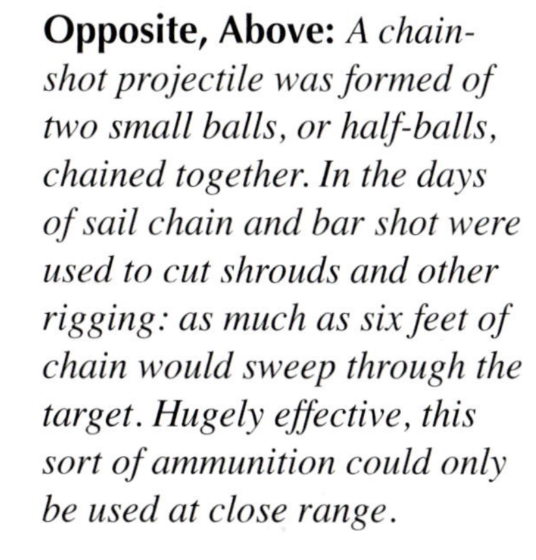

Opposite, Above: *A chain-shot projectile was formed of two small balls, or half-balls, chained together. In the days of sail chain and bar shot were used to cut shrouds and other rigging: as much as six feet of chain would sweep through the target. Hugely effective, this sort of ammunition could only be used at close range.*

Opposite, Below: *Roger Fenton's images of the Crimean War in 1855 heralded the start of real war photographers. This shows mortar batteries in front of Picquet house.*

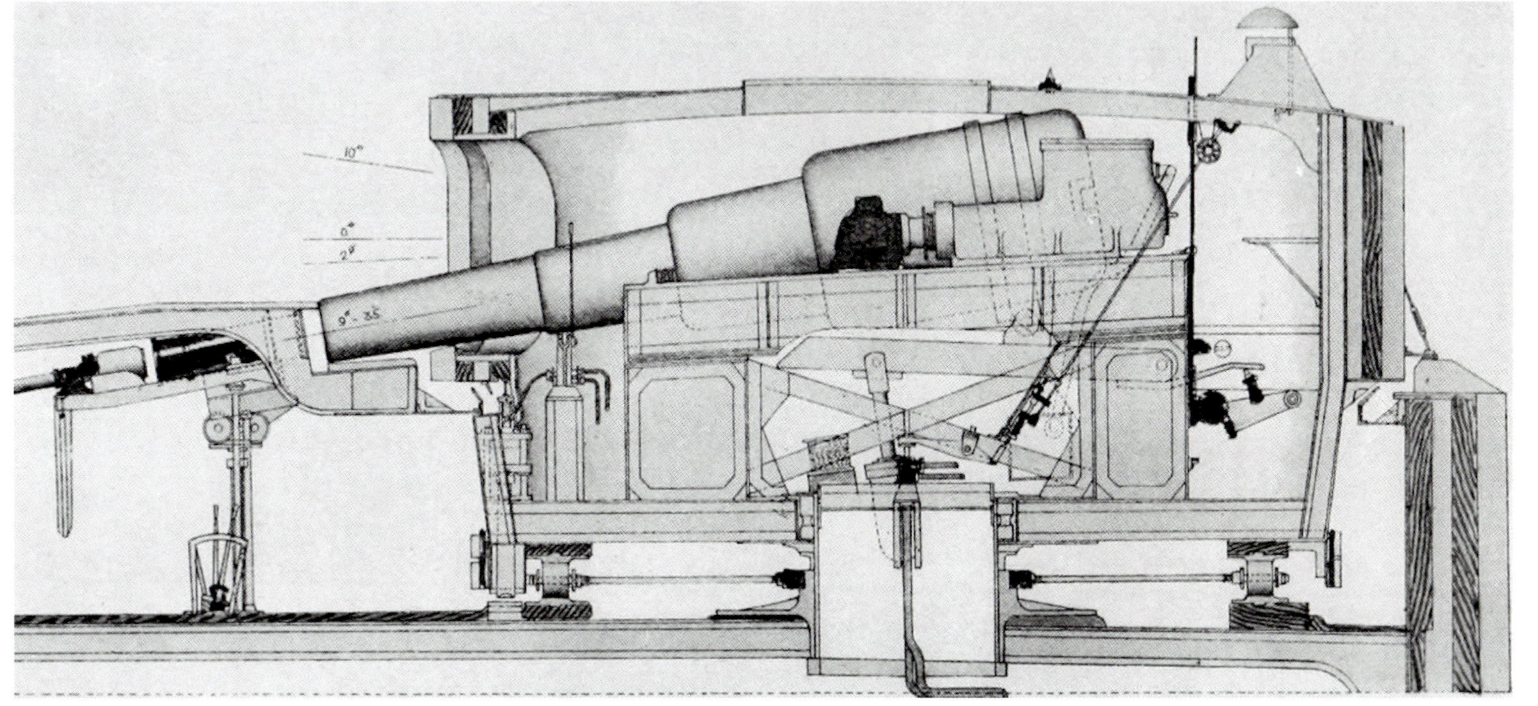

Left: *A diagram showing the complex loading arrangements for the 16-inch RML installed aboard HMS* Inflexible *in 1876.*

As far as armor was concerned, it was not possible to provide the required weight and thickness over the whole ship, and the concept of the central-battery ship became popular. Here, fewer but heavier guns were mounted on the broadside in a central armored citadel amidships. The merit of this system over the rotating turret was hotly debated and the introduction of new technology was by no means a simple matter. In 1870 the Royal Navy commissioned HMS *Captain*, a ship-rigged steamship armed with four 12-inch MLs in two turrets. After only a few months *Captain* capsized in a gale with the loss of almost 500 lives. As long as a full sailing rig was seen to be necessary it was difficult to site turrets where they had a good field of fire and did not interfere with the running of the ship. Eventually it was accepted that sails were no longer necessary and HMS *Devastation* (launched 1871) was the first British battleship to rely on steam power alone. Armed with four 12-inch RML in twin turrets fore and aft she set the basic shape for most of the Royal Navy's battleships for the next thirty years although several later classes carried their main armament in open barbettes rather than enclosed turrets.

Below: *The interrupted-screw breech mechanism. Although in this case shown on a small-caliber 4-inch gun, the principle of operation applies to the larger calibers.*

The Armstrong breech-loading guns of 1861 had proved unsatisfactory and muzzle-loaders continued to arm Royal Navy battleships until around 1880, including HMS Inflexible (launched 1876) which mounted four 16-inch RML. However, from 1882 onward breech-loading guns utilizing the interrupted-screw method were used exclusively for subsequent construction. These guns also adopted slow-burning powders for propellant charges and required longer barrels to make the most effective use of the new compounds. This was facilitated by the introduction of steel into the gun-making process resulting in barrels which were both lighter and stronger. Throughout the latter half of the 19th century British developments were very much influenced by foreign trends, particularly those of France and Italy. Indeed French engineers were responsible for most of the technical advances in guns, ammunition, and explosives while between 1873 and 1882 Italy commissioned the two "Caio Dulio" class ironclads each armed with four 17.7-inch RML—the largest of their type ever mounted in a warship.

Between 1882 and 1910 the Royal Navy adopted the 12-inch BL which eventually became its standard heavy gun and was produced in several progressively improved versions until superseded by larger caliber weapons prior to the outbreak of war in 1914. Virtually every other major navy including those of the United States, France, Italy, Japan and Russia also utilized the 12-inch/305mm gun during this period.

This Page: *By the end of the 19th century the 12-inch BL gun had been widely adopted by most of the major navies. This shows a twin 12-inch/305mm turret carried aboard the French pre-Dreadnought* Justice*, launched in 1904.*

Forts and Castles: The United States

Below: *Fort McHenry was armed with 18-pdr, 24-pdr and 32-pdr cannon when bombarded in 1814. Today 15-inch Rodman smoothbores of Civil War vintage with rifled inserts can be found on the ramparts.*

The French, British, and Spanish built many forts in America to defend their colonies against each other and the Native Americans. Just as in Europe, these started as wooden structures and grew in sophistication and complexity, all the time reflecting the specific requirements of their location. The style of fortification, unsurprisingly, was the same as in Europe with star forts initially giving way to more artillery-conscious designs. Following the Revolutionary War, the United States inherited many locations and built others. Many of these were to defend the seacoast. There were three distinct period of seacost fortification building prior to the Civil War: the First System (1794–1801) saw twenty forts built; the Second System (1802–1815) got going when war with Britain threatened. Many of these forts included casemated guns to protect the crews from airburst shrapnel. Included among them was Fort McHenry, the bombardment of which in 1814 led to the Star-Spangled Banner national anthem. The Third System followed the War of 1812 as Congress provided $800,000 and surveyed many sites—by 1850 some 200 had been recommended. In the end forty-two protecting important harbors were built or under construction as the Civil War started: a number of earlier structures were upgraded—McHenry benefited from improvements with the addition of outer works.

Below: *Castillo de San Marcos near St. Augustine, FL has a long and varied history. Built by the Spanish, it is the oldest masonry fort in the continental United States. It was twice besieged unsuccessfully by the British (in 1702 and 1740) before being ceded in 1763 as part of the Treaty of Paris ending the Seven Years' War (known as the French and Indian War in America). After the Revolutionary War it became Fort Marion and after the Civil War it was used as a prison. It reverted to its original Spanish name after approval by Congress in 1942 and subsequently came under the National Parks Service. The fort is essentially square with four bastions on the corners. It originally had some limited outer works and a moat. After the Revolutionary War a water battery was placed over the old eastern moat. On the eve of the Civil War, the fort's heavy artillery included four 8-inch seacoast howitzers and sixteen 32-pdr seacoast guns. This had dwindled to three 32-pdr guns and two 8-inch seacoast howitzers, along with "a number of very old guns…."*

This Spread: *Fort Jefferson at the Dry Tortugas. Construction of the fort began in December 1846. Each tier of casemates in this huge brick structure housed 150 guns, and another 150 were placed on top of the fort itself. Used as a prison during the Civil War, the seawall was only completed in 1872 when six 15-inch Rodman guns were in place on barbette (third) tier.*

Below: *To allow cannon to be fired over a parapet rather than through an embrasure, the "barbette" carriage was devised. As can be seen, the gun is on a traversable mounting, with a large wheel for handling. This allowed the crew to roll the truck forward on the support. Here, soldiers with 24-pdr siege gun on a wooden barbette carriage at Fort Corcoran, Arlington, VA.*

Left: *After Atlanta fell the Union built new defenses. This is Federal Fort No. 9, in November 1864 as photographed by George N. Barnard, official photographer for the Military Division of the Mississippi, who accompanied Sherman's army on its invasion of Georgia.*

Above: *A taste of things to come. The view from the parapet of the Confederate works in front of Petersburg, VA, showing gabions, bombproofs, "chevaux de frise," and rifle pits in the distance—it's not far off the trenches of World War I.*

This Spread: *The "Gibraltar of Chesapeake Bay" resulted from the War of 1812 when it became obvious that the United States had to protect its harbors and navigable waterways from an enemy fleet. In March 1819, President James Monroe appointed a Board of Engineers for Fortifications who identified the locations that needed defending and work soon started. The President's involvement was recognized when Fort Monroe took his name. Completed in 1834, the United States' largest stone fort boasted a number of 32-pdrs. In conjunction with Fort Calhoun this meant the entrance to the bay was covered. Fort Monroe wasn't the first fort here. In 1609 the Jamestown colonists built Fort Algernon. The area is steeped in history: the first Africans—indentured servants—were unloaded here, effectively the start of slavery in North America; the second oldest lighthouse in the bay was erected here in 1803; Robert E. Lee was stationed here 1831–1834; the battle of Hampton Roads took place in the bay beyond; President Abraham Lincoln was a guest in May 1862; Jefferson Davis was kept here 1865–1867; and in 1907 the Coast Artillery School was set up here. Today, overlooking the parade ground can be found the Lincoln Gun—a 15-inch Rodman that fired a 437lb solid-shot projectile (***Left***). Forged in 1860 it reached Fort Monroe in March 1861—it's 15ft 10in long and 4ft in diameter.*

Opposite, Far Left: *The Third System Fort Point, San Francisco, was finished in 1861. Today it is dwarfed by the Gold Gate Bridge. The three-tiers of casemates and upper level housed 103 cannon which were out of date and scrapped by the end of the 19th century.*

Left: *This 1917 photograph shows the emplacement for the first type of disappearing gun in the United States, a 15-inch Rodman on King's depression carriage. So-called because the gun was moved down behind the parapet by the force of its own recoil, it was part of Fort Wadsworth's Battery Hudson.*

Above: *Originally named Fort Richmond, this is Battery Weed, part of Fort Wadsworth on Staten Island. Like Fort Point, it is a Third System fort with three tiers of casemates and an upper level with 116 cannon facing to seaward. There were also twenty-four flank howitzers on the landward front.*

Above Right: *Aerial view of Battery Cheney on Corregidor, a World War II gun emplacement with two M1895 12-inch coastal guns on disappearing mounts.*

Right: *USS* New Jersey *passes between Corregidor and Fort Drum's 14-inch gun turrets as she enters Manila Bay.*

GRIBEAUVAL'S 12-INCH MORTAR

18th Century
France
Designer: Jean-Baptiste de Gribeauval
Manufacturer: Berenger

Barrel length: 3ft 8in
Weight: 1.7 tons
Caliber: 325mm (12.8 inches)
Max range: 1,695yd

1778: Gribeauval's 12-inch Mortar

In France artillery officer and engineer Jean-Baptiste de Gribeauval became the first inspector of artillery in 1776 and set about reforming the production of his country's cannon, concentrating on three basic types, for use in the field, sieges, or coastal defense. He began to standardize and prefabricate more precise parts, including the shells and the amount of propellant each shot used. Gribeauval strengthened his cannon by starting with a single solid block cast iron which was then carefully drilled out, making a more precise bore and allowing the weapon to be shorter barreled and lighter without sacrificing its range or accuracy. He also designed an improved gun carriage for rapid movement around rough battlefields, with a limber and caisson for crew and ammunition and used horses in pairs—a team of six for the gun and a team of four for each ammunition caisson. His new guns were used in the French Revolutionary War and paved the way for Napoleon Bonaparte's radical artillery tactics in his European wars. They also saw service in the American War of Independence with General Rochambeau's French expeditionary corps, from 1780–1782.

His 12-inch mortar, Mortier de 12 Pouces, (a "pouce" being approximately an inch) was used as siege artillery. Cast of bronze it required a crew of fifteen men and six horses. Initially it had a cylindrical chamber but in 1789 the Gomer conical chamber was incorporated. Some of the Mortier de 12 pouces were also used in coastal defenses, where they were attached to metal platforms.

Left: Obusier *(howitzer) de 6 pouces Gribeauval.*

Below: *Gribeauval coastal 12-inch mortar of 1806.*

1779: RN 68-pdr Carronade

This weapon takes its name from the Carron ironworks in Scotland where it was invented and subsequently produced in sizes to fire shot from 6lb to 68lb. By using a substantially reduced charge the weight and length of the barrel was much reduced making for a much lighter gun effective only at short ranges. This was not necessarily a great disadvantage in an era when naval engagements were mostly fought at very close quarters. Their light weight meant that they could be mounted in relatively small vessels and potentially, for example, a frigate armed with carronades could have the same weight of broadside as a ship-of-the-line. The gun was normally mounted on a slide carriage attached to a pivot mounting on the ship's side allowing a considerable degree of traverse, and elevation was by means of a screw jack under the cascable. Introduced into the Royal Navy in 1779, the most common versions were the 32 and 24-pdrs but the largest was the 68-pdr which in total weighed 35cwt (3,920lb)—two of which were carried by HMS *Victory* and some other first rates and which was credited with a range of 1,280 yards. Ships of the time were rated according to the number of guns they carried but initially carronades were not counted for this purpose although by the early 19th century they were so popular that many smaller ships such as frigates were armed entirely with carronades.

Left: *French Carronade at Rochefort. The Arsenal de Rochefort was set up by Louis XIV in 1665 and fortified by Vauban. It closed in 1926.*

68 Pounder Carronade
Short lightweight gun that fired a heavy round shot at low velocity over a short range. Invented by General Robert Melville and first manufactured by Charles Gascoigne of the Carron Ironworks, Stirlingshire, Scotland in 1778, this type of gun was introduced into the navy in 1779. Carronades came in a variety of sizes: 12, 18, 24, 32 and 68 pounders. It was unusual to have the heavier 68 pounder type mounted on a ship, Victory being the only ship at the battle to carry them.
Weight of gun
Weight of shot
Weight of charge
Range - point blank
Range - maximum

1832: The Monster Mortar

The muzzle-loading Monster Mortar (*Mortier Monstre*, Leopold, or Liège Mortar) was designed by the French artillery officer Henri-Joseph Paixhans (inventor of the first delayed-mechanism shell-firing guns) and was ordered by the Belgian war Minister Baron Empain to help his country secede from the Spanish controlled Netherlands. It was made of cast iron at the Belgian royal foundry in Liège, Belgium in 1832.

It fired 1,100lb bombs of both solid and explosive-shell round-shot and was used in action during the siege of Antwerp in 1832, from November 15–December 23, when it was launched against the city from the citadel, but was damaged and abandoned in Fort Montebello soon after the battle. It later exploded during a test-firing on May 18, 1833 and a second monster mortar was manufactured in Liège in 1834.

Left: *A 68-pdr carronade on a typical slide and pivot mounting.*

Below: *The Great Liège or Monster Mortar employed during the siege of the citadel at Antwerp in 1832.*

THE MONSTER MORTAR

19th Century
Belgium
Designer: Henri-Joseph Paixhans
Manufacturer: Royal Foundry, Liége, Belgium
Location: None extant

Barrel length: 22ft
Weight: 8.5 tons
Caliber: 610mm (24 inches)
Range: 1,000yd

1847: Royal Navy 68-pdr Cannon

ROYAL NAVY 68-PDR (COMMON VARIANT)

19th Century
Great Britain
Designer: Col. William Dundas
Manufacturer: Low Moor Iron Works, Bradford, England
Location: Various surviving including Fort Nelson, Hampshire, England; Bradleys Head, Sydney Harbour, Australia

Barrel length: 9ft 7in
Weight: 5.3 tons
Caliber: 206mm (8.1 inches)
Max range: 3,000yd

During and after the Napoleonic Wars the standard heavy gun aboard Royal Navy ships was the muzzle-loading smoothbore 32-pdr cannon. In 1841 Colonel William Dundas designed a 68-pdr smoothbore cannon which entered service in 1847. The most common variant weighed 95cwt (just under 4 tons) and had an effective range of around 3,000 yards although this could be increased to 3,620 yards if the barrel was elevated to fifteen degrees—something that was rarely done aboard ship. The gun was normally mounted on the traditional four-wheeled truck controlled by ropes and tackle to absorb the recoil and run out the gun after loading although by the time of the Crimean War a slide mounting had been introduced for bowchasers and quarterdeck guns. The coming of iron-hulled ships such as HMS *Warrior* allowed for the carriage of more heavy guns and her armament included no less than twenty-eight 68-pdr ML mounted on the broadside. Subsequently, a further ten armored frigates included the 68-pdr ML as part of their main armament but from 1867 onwards these were all replaced by new 7-inch RML. Although the day of the smoothbore cannon was effectively over, many of the 2,000 68-pdrs produced were bored out and fitted with a rifled liner which enabled them to fire an 80lb solid shot or explosive shell. Most of these were deployed for coastal defense purposes and in this role some remained in service until as late as 1921.

Left: *A 68-pdr muzzle-loading cannon on a slide mounting aboard HMS* Sidon, *a steam-powered paddle frigate, in action off Sebastopol during the Crimean War (1854–1855).*

Right: *An example of the widely used 32-pdr on display in the Gibraltar garrison.*

1857: Mallet's Mortar

Mallet's Mortar has the distinction of being one of the two largest superguns by caliber ever built—the other, Little David Mortar, was made in the US a century later. It was designed by Robert Mallet, who came from a famous family of iron-founders in Dublin. His mortar was designed in 1854 for the reduction of the massive fortifications of Sebastopol during the Crimean War (1853–1956). However, due to the bankruptcy of the company initially chosen by the Government and necessity of spreading the work out amongst other firms, the two mortars commissioned were not completed before that conflict ended. One mortar underwent trials in 1857, being fired a total of nineteen times in a series of four tests, each of which was halted by damage to the weapon. Though Mallett's concept was sound, the metallurgical, engineering, and chemical propellant skills of the time were insufficient. Neither of the mortars were ever used in action.

Realizing that transport would be one of the key problems, Mallet designed his cast-iron mortar in nine main components that could be transported separately and then assembled on site. The barrel and breech consisted of five parts that slotted into each other and were then held together with four massive longitudinal bracing iron staves or straps held with thick hoops at each end. The gun was designed to sit on a timber bulwark and earth frame that would set its elevation at the optimum 45°. The munitions made for the mortar, muzzle-loaded by crane, were both shell and shot cast-iron balls weighing over a ton, ranging from 2,352lb to 2,940lb, and used an 80lb firing charge of propellant with a range of over a mile and a half. Both mortars have survived and can be seen in Woolwich, London and Fort Nelson, Portsmouth.

Left: *Mallet's Mortar, a very large mortar of which only two were built. This one stands on Greenhill Terrace, Woolwich, South East London. It is on loan from the Royal Armouries.*

MALLET'S MORTAR

19th century
Great Britain
Designer: Robert Mallet
Manufacturers: Horsfall & Co, London; Fawcett, Liverpool; Preston & Co, Liverpool
Location: Royal Armouries, Portsmouth and Royal Artillery, Woolwich, England

Barrel length: 11ft
Weight: 47.4 tons
Caliber: 914mm (36 inches)
Max range: 1.5 miles
Artillery, Woolwich

1860: US Dahlgren Shell Guns

DAHLGREN SHELL GUNS

19th Century
United States
Designer: John A. Dahlgren
Location: Various surviving: IX-inch Dahlgren, Washington Navy Yard; XV-inch Dahlgren at Hong Kong Museum of Coastal Defense

Barrel length: up to 20 inches
Weight: 4 to 7 tons
Caliber: 9-inch to 20-inch (IX to XX)
Max range: 3,650 yards

Rear Admiral John A. Dahlgren (1809–1870) gave his name to a series of patented muzzle-loading guns whose distinctive curved shape resulted from a scientific study of the stresses imposed on a gun by the expanding propellant gasses as it was fired. Naturally the heaviest casting was around the breech, tapering off in proportion to the stresses experienced towards the muzzle. These weapons were capable of firing both shell and solid shot to a greater range than conventional cannon. Initially produced in a 32-pdr version for river gunboats, Dahlgren later developed larger weapons in IX-inch, X-inch and XI-inch calibers (for some reason Roman numerals were adopted to describe these guns) which were used by both sides during the American Civil War (1861–1865). In the famous engagement between the USS *Monitor* and the CSS *Virginia* (ex-*Merrimack*) the former mounted two XI-inch Dahlgrens in a revolving turret, while the latter included six IX-inch Dahlgrens in broadside mountings. The ability of the Dahlgren guns to fire solid armor-piercing shots made them extremely useful in this early ironclad period.

The 4-ton IX-inch gun fired a 90lb shot to a range of 3,450 yards while the 7-ton XI-inch gun fired a 166lb shot to the slightly greater range of 3,650 yards. Later developments included the 18-ton XV-inch gun produced in long and short versions which fired a 440lb shot although range is listed only as 2,100 yards as the gun could not be elevated above seven degrees. Ultimately four XX-inch Dahlgrens were produced between 1864 and 1867 and these fired a 1,080lb shell although they did not see any operational service with the US Navy. The XV and XX-inch guns were produced using the patented hollow-casting method devised by Thomas Jackson Rodman and consequently were sometimes confusingly referred to as Rodman guns.

Left: *While designed primarily for naval use, Dahlgren guns were also used on land. Here, Confederate water battery in the defensive lines around Yorktown armed with Dahlgren XI-inch smoothbore naval guns on Marsilly carriages, which had only one set of "trucks" or wheels.*

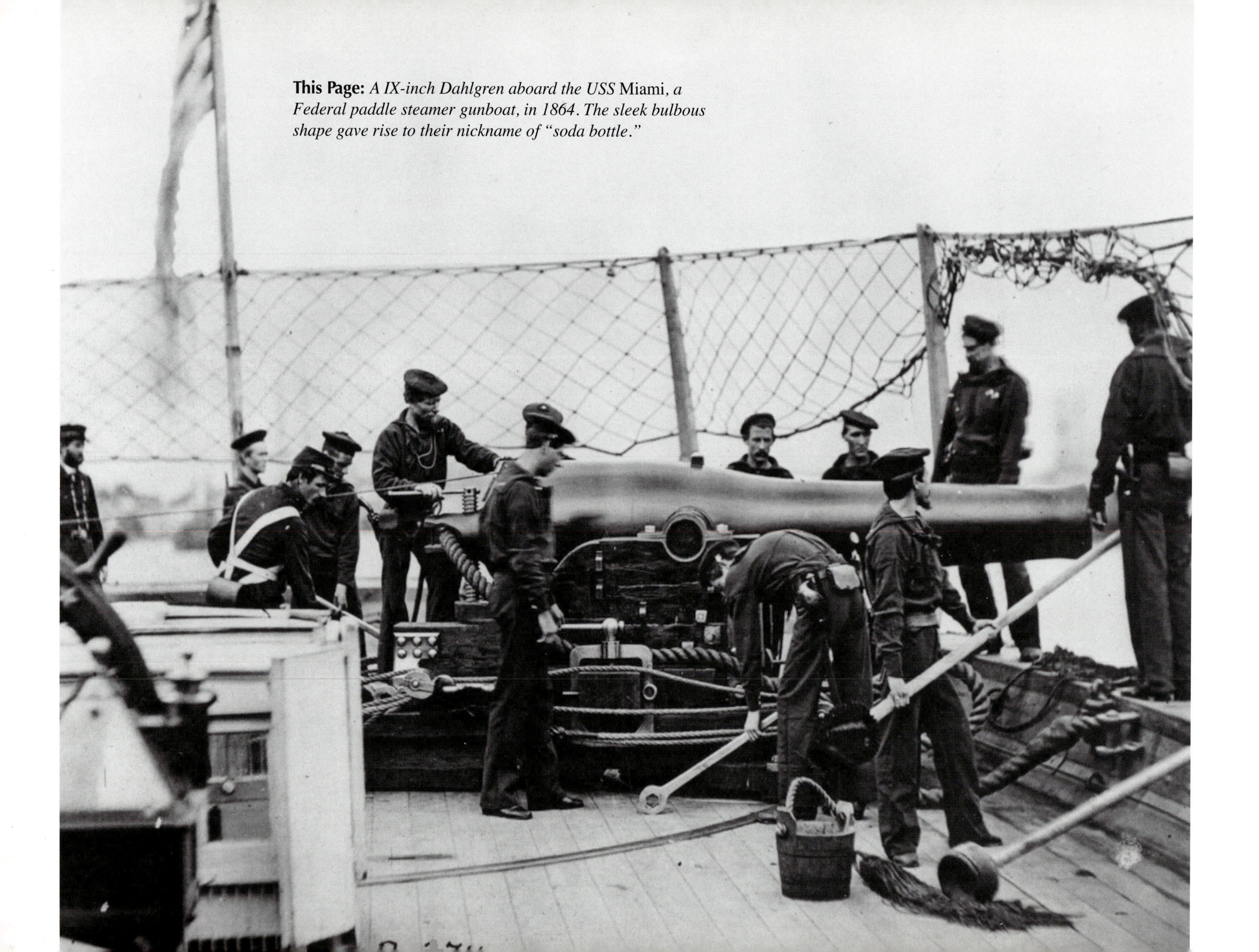

This Page: *A IX-inch Dahlgren aboard the USS* Miami, *a Federal paddle steamer gunboat, in 1864. The sleek bulbous shape gave rise to their nickname of "soda bottle."*

1861: US 13-inch Seacoast Mortar

The Union seacoast mortars were the heaviest of their kind and the 13-inch version saw regular action during the American Civil War, being used by both the army and the navy. Whether mounted on ships or used in batteries in sieges against fortifications or to suppress enemy artillery on land, it proved itself to be an effective weapon. It was manufactured exclusively at the Fort Pitt Foundry, Pittsburgh between 1860 and 1864 out of cast iron, with a barrel length of 4.7ft and a weight of 17,250lb. It fired 200lb round explosive shells which were loaded using a pole-frame crane, with a propellant charge of 14–20lb. One of the most famous 13-inchers was known as *Dictator*. It was of critical importance in the 1864 siege operations against Petersburg, VA. Placed on flatbed railroad car the mortar then used the existing railroad tracks to get closer to the city, from where it could bombard at will, causing widespread damage and destruction, degrading defenses, destroying shelters and weapon stores. Served by Company G of the 1st Connecticut Heavy Artillery its main mission was harassing enemy artillery—in particular Chesterfield Battery across the Appomattox River. During the Battle of the Crater on July, *Dictator* fired nineteen rounds in support of the Union attack to great effect. One shell destroyed a cannon and another shell killed a number of men in the Chesterfield Battery.

13-INCH SEACOAST MORTAR

19th Century
United States
Maker: Fort Pitt foundry
Location: Various surviving: Harbor Defense Museum, New York City, NY; Ringwood State Park, NJ

Barrel Length: 4ft 8in
Weight: 8.6 tons
Caliber: 13 inches (330mm)
Max range: 2.4 miles

Left: Dictator *in front of Petersburg October, 1864. Unlike other cannon, mortars didn't have an end knob or cascable with which to maneuver and carry it, instead they had lugs at the breech end and at the top of the barrel to aid lifting and handling. An accurate reproduction of a 13-inch mortar made from the original 1861 plans can be seen today at the Harbor Defense Museum in New York City.*

Left and Below Right: *The fieldworks outside Yorktown were constructed in April 1862. They were the first undertaken by the Army of the Potomac. Battery No. 4 was technically demanding because it was dug into the bank of Wormley's Creek. Capt Wesley Brainerd and the 50th New York Engineers did the work, creating a platform for ten 13-inch mortars. They were manned by 1st Connecticut Heavy Artillery.*

Below: *Another view of* Dictator *at Petersburg.*

Right: *Federal mortar battery on Morris Island with 10-inch Model 1841 seacoast mortars, during the siege of Charleston, 1865. Defended by Fort Wagner, the Union spent some months campaigning to take Charleston. It was against Fort Wagner in July 1863 that the attack of African-American 54th Massachusetts, was repulsed with heavy losses.*

1863: US 10-inch Parrott Rifle

Below, Left and Right: *Famously, the 10-inch Parrott, the only gun in Battery Strong on Morris Island, burst its barrel when a projectile exploded. The burst barrel didn't stop the gun from firing although a subsequent explosion did. It took four men to lift the huge 250lb projectiles into the muzzle-loader which was manned by the 7th Connecticut Infantry with Captain Sylvester Gray in command. Its on a center-pintle carriage.*

In 1861 Capt Robert Parker Parrott patented his "rifle" and by 1863 he was the superintendent at the West Point Foundry in New York producing the guns. His weapons were famous for their range and accuracy and were for the most part reliable. His method of construction was to use a combination of cast and wrought iron, the cast barrel at the breech end being surmounted with a thick reinforcing band of wrought iron which was attached while still molten whilst the gun was rotated while being cooled with water poured down the muzzle. The inside of the barrel was then rifled by lathe. When the civil war started Parrott immediately stopped selling his weapons to the southern states, but copies were made and his rifles became a popular weapon used by both sides. Being primarily cast iron they were not without occasional failure—the famous 8-inch (20.3cm), *Swamp Angel* only managed thirty-six shots into the city of Charleston before its barrel cracked.

The largest Parrott Rifle was the 10-inch 300-pdr, with an overall length of 176 inches and a band five inches thick and thirty-six inches long. It weighed 26,900lb, fired a 300lb shell using a 26lb charge up to 9,000yd. Point Foundry produced forty-two 10-inch Parrotts from June 1863 to April 1866. Of these, thirteen survive today. In addition to an example at Fort Moultrie (**Opposite**), four sit at Fort Jefferson and two more at Fort Taylor in Florida.

10-INCH PARROTT RIFLE

19th Century
United States
Maker: West Point Foundry
Designer: Capt Robert Parker Parrott
Location: Various surviving: including Forts Moultrie, SC, Jefferson, FL, and Taylor, FL

Barrel Length: 13ft
Weight: 13.5 tons
Caliber: 10 inches (254mm)
Max range: 5 miles

Left: *This Parrott 10-inch (300-pdr) is seen at Fort Chatfield, Morris Island. It is named after Colonel Brayton of the 3rd R.I. Heavy Artillery who became a Colonel in 1864. He was Chief of Artillery on the staff of General Gillmore (Department of the South) during the assault on Charleston.*

Above: *10-inch Parrott rifle on display at Fort Moultrie. The band measures thirty-six inches in length. It's five inches thick, and added 5,540lb to the overall weight of 26,900lb.*

This Page: *Established in 1863, Fort Cape Disappointment was activated on April 15, 1864, and renamed Fort Canby on February 13, 1875, after General Edward R.S. Canby, who was killed in the Modoc Indian War. There were three batteries, that were supposed to have a total of twenty-two guns. The Lighthouse Battery had a total of seven guns, two 8-inch, four 10-inch, and one huge 15-inch Rodman smoothbore mounted on a center pintle in front of the lighthouse. Note the barbette mountings of the 10-inch Parrotts closest to the camera. Along with forts Columbia and Stevens, Canby was sited to defend the entrance of the Columbia River.*

This Page: *During the siege of Yorktown, Federal Battery No. 1 mounted a 200-pdr and ten 100-pdr Parrotts. The photograph appeared in Gardner's* Photographic Sketchbook of the War, Vol. II. *The extensive caption places the battery in the orchard of the Farinholt House and says: "The rebels, in trying to return the deadly fire of this artillery, burst one of their largest rifle guns, with fatal effect upon the cannoniers. That the fire of battery 'NUMBER ONE' contributed largely to the reasons for evacuating the stronghold, there can be no doubt, the rebels wisely reasoning that if one battery could accomplish so much, what might not be the result if all opened." Note the barbette mounting and the gabions used to form the revetment.*

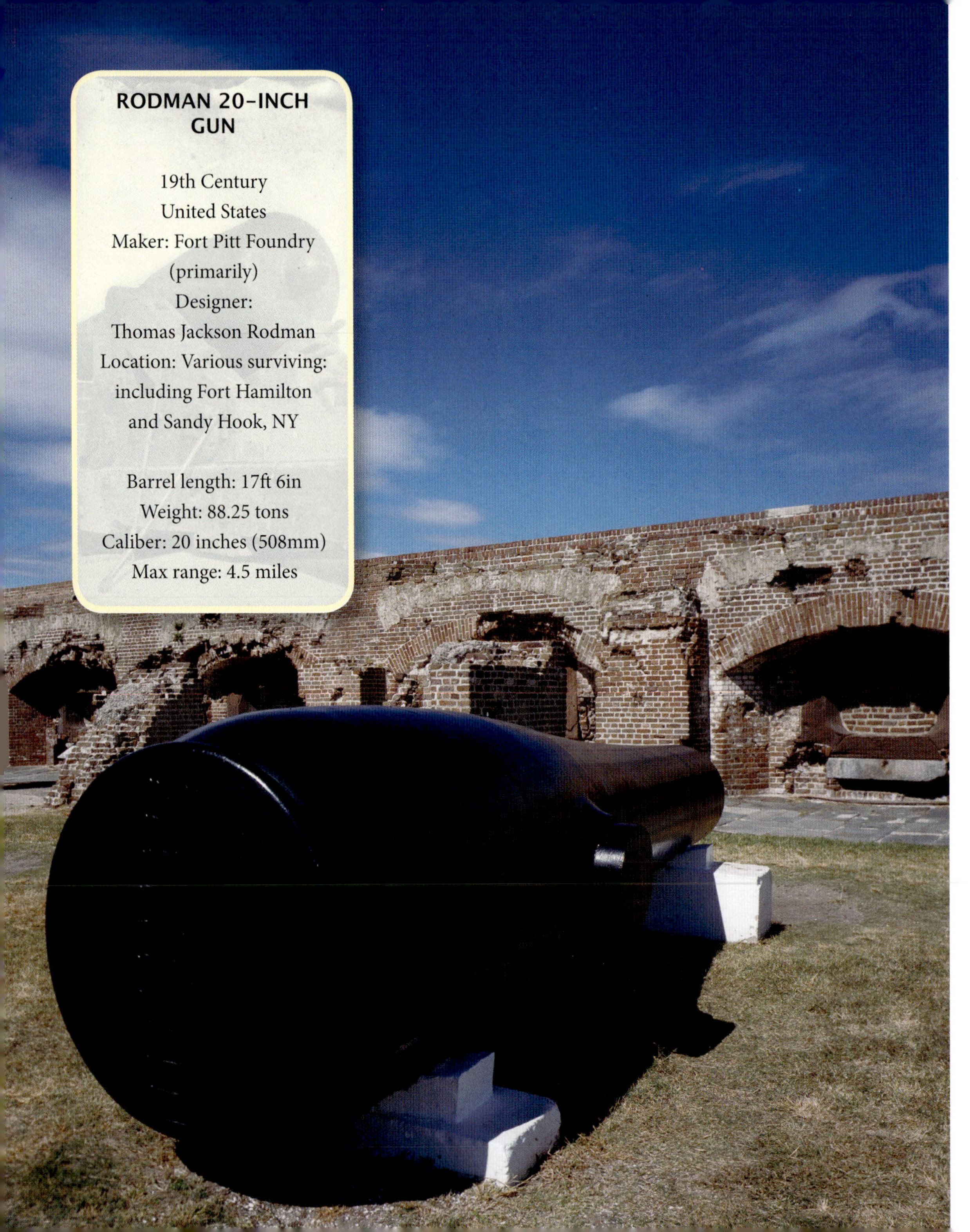

1864: Rodman 15/20-inch Gun

Thomas Jackson Rodman (1815–1871) was an American Union artillery officer whose meticulous research and experimentation lead to various advances in both the construction of artillery and in the propellant which fired their munitions. He went on to build a series of heavy superguns designed for coastal fortifications.

Rodman's radical new manufacturing process was called "hollow cast." Up until that time cannon were cast around solid cores and so could only be cooled from the outside, causing the metal to contract toward the outer surface of the barrel, creating internal strains and structural irregularities in the metal. Thus large guns were all too often prone to cracking during the cooling process or burst when fired. Rodman cast his cannon around a hollow core, cooled from the inside by a carefully controled stream of running water to regulate the temperature, which made the metal contract towards the bore and increased its density. With his system proven and the consequent government approval he began to produce a series of ever larger "Columbiads"—smoothbore, muzzle-loading coastal defense cannon that could fire both solid shot and shell at high and low trajectories.

The first was the 15-inch (38cm). Bulbously bottle-shaped (similar to Armstrong's design), the barrel alone weighed 49,000lb. Two types of ammunition were supplied—a 450lb solid shot, and a 330lb explosive shell carrying a 17lb bursting charge. Rodman went on to build a colossal 20-inch (50.8cm) supergun for Fort Hamilton in New York harbor in 1864, requiring metal from six simultaneous furnaces along with new finishing machinery and transport. The four-piece mold took 160,000lb of molten iron and cooling took nearly a week, after which the gun was finished on a specially built lathe. The completed barrel weighed 116,497lb. Its total length was 20.3ft, with the bore length 17.5ft; thus the bore length to diameter ratio of 10.5 was even lower than that for the 15-inch Rodman gun. Both the shot and the shell for the 20-incher were more than twice the weight of the same projectiles for the 15-inch model, the solid shot weighing 1,080lb, slightly over half a ton, and the explosive shell 725lb empty of the propellant charge. The gun sat on an iron front-pintle barbette carriage weighing 36,000lb.

Rodman's heaviest cannons were fantastic weapons for their time, but from a practical point of view their usefulness was extremely limited. Aiming time depended on the extent of adjustment, but it took too long to traverse the gun 90 degrees. The 20-inch gun required twice the loading and aiming time of the 15-inch gun—too slow for a fast-moving ship. His guns proved his theories, particularly the advantages of progressively burning powder, but the 20-inch gun was still too big to be a really effective weapon.

The guns still exist. Old "No. 1" still sits at Fort Hamilton, now a public park, mounted on a concrete base, and another looks out over New York Harbor from Sandy Hook.

Left: *Around 1,840 Rodman guns were made for the Union, most of them for coastal forts, and few saw action. This 15-incher is at Fort Sumter.*

Above Right: *Confederate Battery Magruder, Yorktown, with 8-inch Rodman Columbiads.*

Right: *8-inch Rodman guns at Fort McHenry.*

1876: Armstrong 17.72-inch Gun

ARMSTRONG 17.72-INCH GUN

19th Century
Great Britain
Designer: William Armstrong
Manufacturers: Elswick Ordnance Company, Newcastle upon Tyne, England

Barrel length: 17.72 inches
Weight: 102 tons
Caliber: 17.72 inches
Max range: 6,600 yards

In 1873 the Italian Navy laid down two new armored turret ships (*Caio Duilio, Enrico Dandolo*) which were to be armed with four 60-ton guns, However, in response to the British HMS *Inflexible* laid down in 1874 which was to carry four 80-ton 16-inch RML, it was decided that the Italian ships would be upgraded to carry four 100-ton 17.72-inch (450mm) RML—the largest muzzle-loading guns ever mounted aboard a ship. These guns were manufactured by the British Armstrong company at their Elswick works on the River Tyne and eleven were ordered by the Italian Navy—four each for the two ships which were completed in 1880 and 1882, and three spares. Each 17.72-inch gun weighed approximately 102 tons, featured a 20.5-cal barrel, and could fire a 2,000lb shell to a maximum of 6,600 yards. The propellant consisted of four or five 112lb shaped charges but during trials with heavier charges one of Duillio's guns fractured and had to

be rebuilt. The guns were mounted in circular turrets position en echelon amidships and operated by hydraulic power, as was the loading cycle. The rate of fire was slow—only one round every four minutes—although the projectile was capable of penetrating 15.5 inches of steel armor plate.

In response to these ships, Britain decided to strengthen the garrison defenses at Malta and Gibraltar and ordered four similar guns which were delivered in 1882–1883. Mounted on hydraulically operated slide carriages, they remained in service until 1906.

Opposite: *This Armstrong 100-ton is one of two which were mounted at Gibraltar in 1883.*

Below: *One of the Armstrong 100-ton RML guns can still be seen at the Napier Battery, Gibraltar. The figure alongside gives some idea of the size of these great weapons.*

1877: Armstrong 100-ton Gun

Below: *Fort Rinella was built on Malta to house an Armstrong 100-ton gun which was placed in position in January 1884. Its mounted en barbette on a wrought-iron sliding carriage.*

Opposite, Inset: *Engraving showing an Armstrong RML 100-ton gun in emplacement and loading arrangements.*

In 1863 Armstrong built his first gun with a core of drilled out, rifled steel enveloped with a wound wire iron jacket of several layers. The success of this sturdy construction spurred on the Government to commission increasingly larger caliber designs from him, culminating in his 100-ton behemoth. However the Royal Navy refused the gun on the grounds primarily of weight and expense so Armstrong was forced to look elsewhere for business. His successful weapons were known and admired worldwide despite a reactionary British response after initial enthusiasm to his radical new breech-loaders. When the Italian Navy commissioned eight of the 100 ton guns for two of their latest battleships the British government, possessing no armaments of that size, was thrown into a panic, in the end ordering the same guns to counterbalance the Italian threat in the Mediterranean. Four guns were made, two for Malta and two for Gibraltar, one of each surviving to this day, on Malta at Fort Rinella and on Gibraltar at Napier of Magdala Battery. The guns necessitated steam-powered hydraulic operating systems to traverse and elevate and as such were some of the first ever mechanically operated weapons. Ultimately they were not particularly successful. They were hideously expensive to fire and because of the requirement of steam power they took some three hours to become operational and their armor-piercing range was only about a mile. Though deemed viable, none of the British guns were ever fired in anger and after twenty years service they were considered obsolete and decommissioned in 1906. In the accelerating arms race of the industrializing nations they had been rapidly superseded by more advanced weapons.

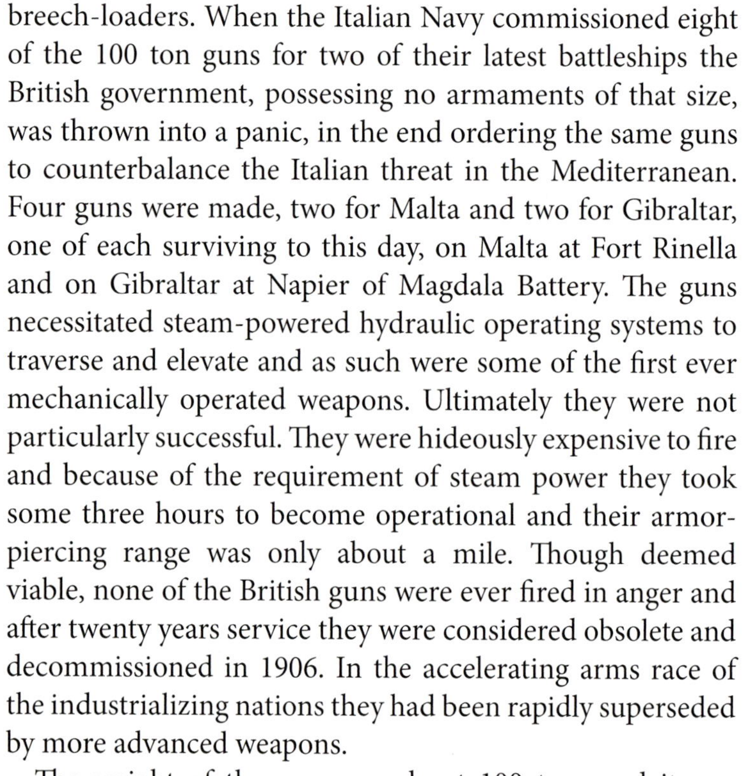

The weight of the gun was about 100 tons and it was operated with a crew of 35 men. It took 441lb of powder propellant to fire its 2,000lb shells (armor-piercing, high explosive or shrapnel) to a maximum range of 3.75 miles. The guns were usually mounted on cast-iron carriages upon raised platforms (en barbette) behind concrete parapets, with revetted side protection.

ARMSTRONG 100-TON GUN

19th Century
Great Britain
Designer: William Armstrong
Manufacturers: Elswick Ordnance Company, Newcastle upon Tyne, England
Location: Fort Rinella, Malta; Napier, Gibraltar

Barrel length: 52.6 feet
Weight: 103 tons
Caliber: 17.7 inches
Crew: 35 men
Max range: 3.75 miles

Left: *The South African Navy Museum fired off an Armstrong gun last fired in service in 1903 and then restored in 2011.*

12-INCH GUN

19th Century
Great Britain
Maker: Vickers
Location: none extant

Barrel length: 50in
Weight: c. 74 tons
Caliber: 12 inches (305mm)
Max range: c. 12 miles

1882: Royal Navy 12-inch Gun

Towards the end of the 19th century the Royal Navy finally began to adopt large-caliber breech-loading guns. The first to carry such weapons were the armored turret ships *Colossus* and *Edinburgh* (1882) which mounted four 12-inch BL Mk. II (the Mk. I designation was applied to guns intended for land use) in two twin turrets amidships and also the battleship *Collingwood* (1882) which carried the four 12-inch guns in open barbette mountings fore and aft—a configuration which became almost standard (although usually with the guns in enclosed turrets) until the advent of HMS *Dreadnought* in 1905. The subsequent use of larger caliber guns such as the 16.25-inch BL and the 13.5-inch BL proved unsatisfactory due to low rates of fire and construction difficulties, so that from 1894 onward the Royal Navy standardized on the 12-inch gun which armed no fewer than forty-nine battleships up to 1910 when larger calibers were adopted. The original Mk. I/II fired a 714lb shell to a range of 9,400 yards, but following a failure during trials aboard HMS *Collingwood* in 1886, these guns were withdrawn and replaced by strengthened versions variously designated Mks. III, IV, or V, although performance remained unchanged.

The "Majestic" and "Canopus" class ships (1894–1899) introduced the 12-inch/35-cal Mk. VII which fired 850–878lb projectiles to a range of 14,680 yards, although longer ranges were achieved by the same gun aboard monitors on mountings which could be elevated to 30 degrees. In 1901 the 12-inch/40-cal Mk. IX gun was introduced. It fired the same shells to a range of 20,950 yards at twenty degrees' elevation and was capable of firing up to two rounds per minute (under ideal conditions) due to improvements in the ammunition handling system. A further increase in barrel length resulted in the 12-inch/45-cal Mk. X gun which armed the revolutionary HMS *Dreadnought* when she entered service in 1906 as well as the subsequent Invincible and "Indefatigable" class battlecruisers. The final iteration of the 12-inch gun was 50-cal Mk. XI and XII which used a heaver 306lb propellant charge in an effort to increase range. However, these guns proved to be inaccurate in range due to incomplete combustion of the charge before the projectile left the barrel demonstrating that the 12-inch gun had reached the limits of its potential and resulted in a trend to larger calibers.

Opposite: *Shells and charges were pushed securely into the breech by this hydraulic ram mechanism.*

Left: *The open breech of a 12-inch gun. This example is actually aboard the American pre-Dreadnought USS* Connecticut *and clearly shows the interrupted screw breech mechanism. Royal Navy 12-inch guns were very similar.*

16.25-INCH GUN MK. I

19th Century
Great Britain
Designer: Elswick Ornance Co
Location: none extant

Barrel length: 43ft 7in
Weight: 110 tons
Caliber: 16.25-inch (412mm)
Max range: 12,000 yards

Below Right: *HMS Benbow at anchor showing the massive "Elswick 110-ton gun" in an open barbette on the forecastle.*

Opposite, Left: *The French coast-defense barbette ship* Requin *(1885) was armed with two 420mm BL guns, the largest caliber ever mounted in a French warship.*

Opposite, Right: *The* Admiral Baudin *was one of two pre-Dreadnoughts which were armed with three 370mm guns mounted fore and aft, and one amidships.*

1885: Royal Navy 16.25-inch Gun

The production of the massive 17.7-inch guns by Armstrongs for the Italian Navy led the Royal Navy to adopt a similar caliber weapon which was subsequently mounted in three battleships launched in 1885–1887. These were 16.25-inch breech-loading guns with a 30-caliber barrel and weighed 110 tons. They were able to fire common (i.e. explosive), shrapnel or armor-piercing shells each weighing 1,800lb (820kg) to a maximum range of 12,000 yards. With such large shells, as well as the fact that the propellant charge weighed 960lb, loading was a slow and complex affair and the best rate of fire was only one round every two and a half minutes. The first ship to be armed with these guns was HMS *Benbow* (1885) which carried two in single open barbette mountings fore and aft, while HMS *Victoria* and HMS *Sans Pareil* (both 1887) had a single armored twin turret forward. Although these guns were among the earliest to utilize steel construction, there were still problems including cracks and barrel droop. Because of this, as various modifications were incorporated, each of the twelve guns actually produced was different. Another problem was barrel wear—a life of only seventy-five firings before they had to be replaced—so any advantage which might have been gained by the adoption of a very large caliber was more than offset by the practical difficulties of their operation. HMS *Victoria* was lost in a notorious incident when she was in collision with HMS *Camperdown* during Mediterranean Fleet maneuvers on June 22, 1893. The other two ships saw relatively little service and were scrapped in 1909, their 16.25-inch guns being something of a dead end in naval gunnery development and were never fired in anger.

1886: French 420mm Modèle 1875 Gun

420MM MODÈLE 1875

19th Century
France
Various builders: Arsenal de Brest, Toulon, Lorient
Location: none extant

Length: 30ft 4in
Weight: 74.8 tons
Caliber: 420mm
Max range: 10,000 yards

The largest French naval gun of the pre-dreadnought era was the massive 420mm Modèle 1875 which armed four so-called coast defense ships, although foreign observers often rated them as seagoing battleships. These ships carried two guns on single mountings in open barbettes fore and aft, each of which had total length of 32.5ft, weighed 74.8 tons and featured a 22-caliber barrel. They could fire a 1,433lb common shell or a 1,719lb armor-piercing shell to around 10,000 yards using a 604lb propellant charge. The four "Terrible" class ships (*Terrible, Caiman, Indomitable, Requin*) were completed 1886–1888 but the problems associated with such large guns (slow rate of fire, handling the heavy shells etc) led them all being refitted in 1898 with smaller 340mm or 274mm guns. A distinctive feature of these ships as completed was their four funnels closely grouped together abaft the bridge. Subsequently the French Navy utilized a variety of heavy guns including a 370mm/28.5 cal (1879) and a 340mm/30-cal (1894) before standardizing on the 305mm/40-cal from 1893 onwards The latter was equivalent to the Royal Navy's 12-inch gun introduced in the "Majestic" class pre-dreadnoughts commissioned from 1895 onward.

DYNAMITE GUN

19th Century
United States
Designer: E.L.G. Zalinski
Location: none extant

Caliber: 15-inch, 381mm
Max range: 1,650 yards

1890 US Navy 15-inch Dynamite Gun

Below and Bottom: *USS* Vesuvius *was specifically designed and built to carry the Dynamite Gun and its associated pneumatic systems. Note the triple breeches of mounted guns at fixed angle of elevation.*

The perfection of high explosives based on stabilized forms of nitroglycerin in the latter half of the 19th century had obvious military applications, but initially it was found that explosives such as dynamite and gelignite were not suitable for use in shells fired from heavy guns: the shock of firing would be enough to trigger the shell with disastrous results. Based on a demonstration by Ohio-based M.D. Medford, the idea of a pneumatic gun was developed by US Army Capt E.L.G. Zalinski. US Navy interest led to the production of a 15-inch gun firing a shell containing up to 600lb of high explosive. A ship specially designed to accommodate such weapons (USS *Vesuvius*) was ordered in 1886 and completed in 1890. Three guns were installed in the forward hull on fixed mountings elevated at 15 degrees and heavy-duty air compressors charged a series of air reservoirs formed from wrought iron tubes. The projectiles were breech-loaded and fired by admitting compressed air at up to 1,000psi into the chamber. Lateral aiming was achieved by altering the ship's heading and range could be varied up to a maximum of 1,650 yards by adjusting the air pressure. As far as it went, the idea was reasonably successful but the fixed mountings and relatively short range made it unsuitable for naval engagements although *Vesuvius* was employed to bombard Santiago, Cuba, during the Spanish–American War of 1898. The material damage caused was insignificant but the dynamite guns had a profound psychological effect as the shells arrived without warning due to the relative quietness of the compressed air discharge. The ship was subsequently placed in reserve and her guns removed in 1904. It is interesting to note that similar weapons were installed in coast defense batteries, including New York and San Francisco, but these were also decommissioned in 1904.

This Page: *The triple barrels of the Dynamite Gun aboard the USS* Vesuvius.

Chapter 3: World War I

Below and Opposite: *From the middle of the 19th century manufacturers, industry, and the military began the "arms race." Driven by technological developments or changes in military thinking, weapons and weapons' platforms got bigger and had to be limited by treaty. Here big guns are made in the Naval Gun Shop, Washington.*

The beginning of the 20th century saw the stage set for a quantum leap in war technology as the industrialized nations vied with each other for supremacy. The standardized arms they mass-produced equipped increasingly massive citizen armies who would experience first hand the increased lethality of these modern weapons. World War I saw the introduction of new technologies—aircraft, tanks, submarines and chemical weapons—but it was the refinement of existing weapons: rifles with magazines, machine-guns, grenades, and above all, artillery that inflicted the most carnage. Artillery's increased lethality originated in the advances of metallurgy, gun design, size, range and ammunition and all these combined to kill more people in the end than any other weapon did.

As the war progressed into a trench stalemate the artillery assets of the opposing armies were greatly increased, becoming larger distinct units in their own right as their use became more critical to mass firepower where it was most needed. Guns were now no longer muzzle-loaders made of smoothbore iron but breech-loaders made of rifled steel, with hydro-pneumatic recoil systems that absorbed the force of the blast and returned the weapon automatically to its firing position, keeping it stable and on target thus increasing its rate of fire. Sights, elevation, and traverse mechanisms became more sophisticated, too. The 1897 French 75mm field gun is considered the first weapon to have had all these attributes and it had a fearsome reputation among the German troops.

Constructing a stable breech-loading firing platform was a crucial first step, another was to develop standardized reliable ammunition which was vital in achieving correct targeting. The consistent manufacture of blast propellant and the weight of the shell were critical and World War I saw the adoption of TNT (Trinitrotoluene) as the primary explosive propellant for artillery shells. It took time for the industries in the competing states to grow the technology and learn the arts of explosive manufacture and consistent munition production. Hard-won knowledge did not come not without catastrophes both at home and on the fronts: this was a total war where civilians were also vital producers of war matériel (and therefore legitimate targets). There were at first many factory accidents, duds, and misfires, but by perfecting their production-line systems and components and training a competent workforce the factories managed for the most part to produce a regular dependable round.

Right: *The Skoda 24cm Mörser M 98 was used by the Austro-Hungarian army, and by the British as Ordnance BL 9.45-inch howitzer Mk. I. The 9.45 led to their nickname of the "Quarter to Ten" guns.*

Below: *The barrel segment of a Skoda 305mm Model 1911 howitzer. The Austro-Hungarian Army loaned eight of these guns to the Germans in August, 1914 and they were used in destroying Belgian fortifications at Liège and other locations.*

Opposite: *Gun shop in the Armstrong Works.*

The British came up with the 106 Fuse shell that detonated on impact with any object instantly—instead of embedding itself first in the earth. This greatly increased the damage such shells could wreak—to people or to blast holes in barbed wire and other defenses.

In ensuring accurate fire other aspects also had to be considered by gunners—the state of their guns needed to be carefully monitored with the measurement of gun barrel wear and tear. The larger the gun, the larger the round—and the larger its charge and their effects on the bore and barrel. The superguns built at this time required regular reboring or changes of barrel after comparatively small numbers of shells had been fired, for they were working on the edge of what was possible. Other considerations were the measurement of wind speed, air pressure and other meteorological factors, taking all these into account when calculating gun settings.

With the larger guns firing indirectly from well beyond line of sight came the problem of accurate targeting. Indirect fire target acquisition is dependent upon correct information and presupposes accurate surveys and maps to produce a proper grid from which to calculate. It also requires forward observation officers, placed forward of the guns to select targets, observe where the shells are landing, or to "blast spot" enemy guns operating and report results back via a communication link (wired field telephone or telegraph). Aerial observation by balloon and aircraft was also used. At the start of the war guns fired a series of initial shots to find the correct range and register on the target but this was a cumbersome process that prevented surprise and gave one's own position away. With time and experience the triangulation of reconnaissance, observation and targeting enabled predictive fire that factored range more precisely.

By such methods artillery's dominance of the battlefield was complete, even when tanks first arrived since they had been rushed into production and were very vulnerable. Tactics evolved using barrages of long duration—either of an enemy's trenches, fortifications, supply and communications areas and fire suppression against his own artillery or a "creeping barrage" in advance of one's own troops to keep the enemy's head down. The war saw the longest continuous barrages the world had ever seen to date, firing mind-boggling quantities of shells for sometimes weeks at a time. They accounted for the majority of the casualties. Out in the open or a direct hit ensured instant demise. Yet despite this, deep bunkers and fortified trenches helped soldiers survive.

Germany had led in the development of heavy weapons, both long-range guns and heavy mortars. They used these to good effect at the start of the war, with a sliding breechblock and metallic cartridge case pioneered by Krupp. They continued to hold the advantage, being the first to construct new superguns. Their original plans had always included the necessity of reducing fortifications but they also recognized the benefits of psychologically intimidating the enemy with the sheer size of a weapon. Their next surprise was a record breaker. The Paris Gun was a monster that could fire shells into the stratosphere and certainly had a demoralizing effect on the city. It was a hybrid based on a heavy naval gun requiring its own custom-built concrete emplacement where it sat on a huge chassis made of railroad trucks on rails, and used the existing rail networks for transport. The logistics of modern warfare made much use of rail systems to move war matériel and troops long distances to railheads near the fronts, where motorized wheel and tracked transport, horses, and manpower then took over. Rail transport was the best method for transporting long-range

superguns and the next development was to just keep them on the rails.

Railroad guns had been first improvised and used in the American Civil War, but World Wars I and II can be considered their heyday. In 1915 the French began what would soon become just this latest aspect of the arms race. The Germans with their passion for bigger and better superguns soon took the lead and these two nations were the main producers and contenders when it came to railroad artillery. All the other major nations followed with their own versions though not in the same quantities. Often using modified naval guns mounted on railroad carriages, these weapons became the largest land guns in the world at the time. For continental Europe they were seen primarily as long-range heavy siege guns, in Britain and the US they were mainly deployed for coastal defense.

At Verdun in 1916 both the Germans and the French massed enormous artillery forces and deployed heavy railroad guns to bombard fortifications, bunker complexes, supply depots, troops concentrations and rear areas. In 1917 at the Third Battle of Ypres two British 14-inch (356mm) railroad guns carried out interdictory bombardments. In 1918 the US initially used five 14-inch railroad guns brought from America but thereafter they were manufactured in France. The war ended with the myth of these superguns intact. Public opinion was perhaps led by patriotic coverage and a belief that is biggest is best. In reality this was not the case—the railroad gun's usefulness did not live up to its reputation. Ultimately given the expense and effort for the amount of shells fired and the casualties caused the conclusion would have to be what is so often the case with superguns—that they aren't worth the effort and you are better off with a greater amount of smaller ones. However for now something of its ancient prestige still lingered.

Below: *Launched in 1906, HMS* Dreadnought *was armed with no fewer than ten 12-inch guns, made all other contemporary battleships obsolete overnight.*

Naval Weapons

At the start of the 20th century the naval arms race triggered by the German desire to build a fleet capable of challenging the Royal Navy was well under way. It was race which Germany could not win and which Britain, with its vast Empire to protect, could not afford to lose. Nevertheless the Royal Navy potentially threw away its commanding lead when it launched the revolutionary HMS *Dreadnought* in 1905. Until then the battleships of both sides had only mounted four heavy guns supported by secondary batteries of varying calibers. By contrast *Dreadnought* was armed with no fewer than ten 12-inch guns and was also the first major warship to be powered by steam turbines giving her a speed advantage of at least three knots over her contemporaries. At a stroke all existing battleships, now classified as pre-dreadnoughts, were rendered obsolete and the starting gun was fired for a new naval arms race. By the time war broke out in 1914 Britain had twenty-nine dreadnought type battleships as well as nine modern battlecruisers while the comparative figures for Germany were seventeen and seven respectively.

It was not only in ship numbers that the Royal Navy held the advantage, but in general its ships were more heavily armed. The first German dreadnought was the SMS *Nassau* launched in 1908 and armed with twelve 280mm (11-inch) guns although subsequent classes mounted 305mm (12-inch) guns. However, by that time the Royal Navy had moved up to a 13.5-inch gun starting with the "Orion" class (laid down 1909–1910) and by 1914 also had the five "Queen Elizabeth" class armed with the new 15-inch gun nearing completion. A similar situation existed in respect of battlecruisers with the German ships mounting 280mm (11-inch) guns although the later "Derfflinger" class did move up to 305mm (12-inch) guns. Nevertheless, the early Royal Navy battlecruisers already carried 12-inch guns while the "Lion" and "Tiger" classes were armed with 13.5-inch guns and *Renown* and *Repulse* (completed in late 1916) carried six 15-inch guns. Germany did commission two 381mm (15-inch) armed battleships in 1916 and also planned 356mm (14-inch) armed battlecruisers which were never completed—but by the end of the war in 1918 Britain had already produced a powerful 18-inch gun in small numbers and was planning new capital ships to be armed with 16-inch guns.

Of course, theory did not always work out in practice. At the battle of Jutland (May 31, 1916) the German battlecruisers decisively outgunned their British opponents, three of which blew up and sank after hits on their turrets caused flash fires which reached the magazines. In addition post-battle analysis showed that a significant proportion of the British armor-piercing shells exploded on contact rather than after penetrating armor as they were designed to do. One informed observer calculated that, based on the number of hits actually obtained, as many as six additional German capital ships might have been sunk if the shells had not malfunctioned.

Above: *USS* Mississippi *was a "New Mexico" class battleship completed in 1917. She subsequently served in World War II during which her guns were removed for relining as shown in this c. 1944 image.*

Although France entered the war as a major naval power, the demands on resources for the bitter land battles meant that only seven dreadnoughts were completed between 1914 and 1918. These were armed with 305mm (12-inch) and later 340mm (13.4-inch) guns although the projected "Normandie" class (none of which were completed) would have been armed with no fewer than sixteen 13.4-inch guns in four quadruple turrets. In common with most European navies, the US Navy initially standardized on the 12-inch gun for its dreadnought battleships but by 1914 it had moved up to 14-inch guns, first mounted in the "New York" class launched in 1912. Subsequently all US battleships completed or laid down during World War I carried ten, and later twelve, 14-inch guns.

1889: Krupp Coastal and Fortress Guns

COASTAL GUN 240MM L/35

19th Century
Germany
Manufacturers: Krupp
Location: Various extant, see photos

Length: 27ft 6in
Weight: 1.95 tons (barrel)
Caliber: 240mm (11-inch)
Max range: 6,500 yards

Krupp was the largest weapons' manufacturer in Europe—if not the world—in the latter years of the 19th and first half of the 20th century. The company began to make steel cannons in the 1840s—especially for the Russian, Turkish, and Prussian markets. Indeed, their export market was immense: by the time Alfred Krupp died in 1887 *der Kanonenkönig* (the Cannon King) had manufactured nearly 25,000 guns; most for the Prussian or German government but more than half for export to nearly fifty countries.

Large coastal artillery played a significant role in this export market, which continued on under Alfred's successors, Friedrich Alfred—"Fritz"—and Gustav. Just to mention a few, these included 1893's 280mm, 1901's 283mm L/40, 1907's 283mm *Küstenhaubitze* (coastal howitzer), 1909's 283mm L/45, 1908's 173mm SK L/40, 1910's 240mm L/35 and 283mm SK L/50, 1914's 240mm SK L/40 and 356mm SK L/52.5.

Today examples of these coastal guns can be found all over the world, a number of which saw action in the world wars: 1893 280mm at the Oscarsborg Fortress in Oslo Fjord (see p.108); 280mm at the Hulishan Fortress of Xiamen, China; 1888 240mm at Rumeli Mecidiye in the Dardanelles (see p. 109); 1889 355mm at the Harbiye Military Museum in Istanbul (Right); 1877 280mm at Suomenlinna fortress, Helsinki, Finland (see p. 109); four 240mm L/35 in Battery No. 4 of Base Naval Puerto Belgrano in Argentina.

Right: *Krupp 240mm L/35 fortress gun in the Military Museum of the Chinese People's Revolution, Beijing, China.*

Left: *This Krupp 335mm L/35 cannon served in the Ottoman army in Gallipoli. Today it is displayed in the Military Museum in Istanbul. The bronze statue is of Corporal Seyit (see p. 109) although the gun he serviced was actually a 240mm.*

FORTRESS GUN
355 L/35

19th Century
Germany
Maker: Krupp
Location: Harbiye Military Museum, Istanbul, Turkey

Barrel Length: 40ft 9in
Weight: 85 tons
Caliber: 355mm (14 inches)
Max range: 10.5 miles

Left and Above: *The guns of Oscarsborg Fortress in Oslofjord, under command of Oberst Birger Eriksen, were instrumental in the sinking of the German heavy cruiser* Blücher *on April 9, 1940. The fortress's armament—a torpedo-tube battery and three Krupp 280mm guns—performed perfectly even though handled by a partly green crew. The battle involved a number of the Norwegian batteries. First, the battery on Rauøy spotted the convoy and fired warning shots. When the Germans did not respond, it fired more shots but missed. The next battery to engage was that of Bolærne, which also fired a warning shot.* Blücher *kept going to reach Oslo by dawn, passing close by Oscarsborg whose 280mm guns hit the* Blücher *twice before 533mm torpedoes launched from North Kaholmen Island finished the job. Around 700 Germans perished when* Blücher *capsized and sank.*

Above and Above Right: *Kilitbahir is on the Gallipoli peninsula opposite Çanakkale. They dominate the straits and were heavily involved in the World War I naval battle that raged between February 17 and March 18, 1915. On March 18 the Anglo-French fleet launched its main attack. During the battle, the shell hoist that served the Krupp 240mm gun in the battery at the Rumeli Mecidiye Rampart went out of service. Cpl Seyit, a timber cutter, famous in his village for his great strength and capable of walking around with a log under each arm, carried a number of 600lb shells to his gun. The shell he holds in the statue (just visible at left, also see the one on p. 107) is probably meant to be the last the battery had on that day. The myth is that it hit and sank the British battleship HMS* Ocean, *but it's likely the warship struck a mine. Turkey bought at least 30 L/35 240mm guns in the 1880s for coastal defense.*

Right: *Krupp 1870 280mm gun in foreground at Suomenlinna fortress; in background at right a Russian license-built copy, made at the Perm Ironworks in 1879.*

1893: Krupp's *Thunderer*

KRUPP'S THUNDERER

19th Century
Germany
Designer: Alfred Krupp
Manufacturers: Krupp, Essen

Barrel length: 46 feet
Weight: 240,000lb
Caliber: 420mm
(16.54 inches)
Max range: 13 miles

In Germany at the family firm of Essen iron founders, Alfred Krupp concentrated on developing cannon made from cast steel, producing his first one in 1847. In 1851 at the Great Exhibition in Britain he exhibited a 4,300lb 6-pdr gun made from a single solid steel ingot, and four years later at the Paris Exhibition of 1855 he displayed a 100,000lb weapon made the same way. He then topped that with his supergun built for the Chicago World Trade Fair in 1893.

The *Thunderer* was the world's biggest gun at the time, its barrel weighed just over 240,000lb and was 46 feet long, 6ft 6in in diameter at the breech and 16.54 inches at the muzzle. It was capable of firing a 2,000lb shell to a range of thirteen miles. The shrapnel version of the one-ton shell was filled with 3,400 steel balls weighing about 0.25lb each.

Besides the Prussian army, both Russia and the Ottoman Empire were regular customers and over time bought thousands of Krupp guns. They sold well in the Balkans and eastern Europe too. Krupp also learned from the Japanese who had dismantled and transported some of their very large coastal defense guns for use in the siege of Port Arthur during the Russo–Japanese war (1904–1905) and he began work on a series of transportable heavy mortars and howitzers, ranging from 280mm to 305mm (11–12-inch) in caliber, based on his coastal defense mortars such as the 1897 305mm (12-inch) Beta-Gerät. A new superior version of the Beta-Gerät was developed in 1908, but still wasn't considered powerful enough by the government so Krupp went on to produce a 420mm (16.5-inch) version with the colossal L/16 16-caliber Gamma-Gerät howitzer, a massively scaled-up version of the Beta. (See p. 118.)

Right: *The great Krupp guns in the Krupp Building of the 1893 Chicago World's Fair. The German firm Krupp had a pavilion of artillery,*

Opposite: *A 1915 scene in the Krupp Gun Works, where so many of Germany's army and navy guns were manufactured. The first Krupp arrived in Essen in 1587 and by the time of the Thirty Years' War the gunsmiths were producing a thousand gun barrels a year. The family cast steel factory was founded in 1811 and its guns helped Prussia defeat Austria in 1866.*

1911: Škoda 305mm M11/M16 Mortar

305MM M11/M16 MORTAR

20th Century
Austria-Hungary
Maker: Skoda-Werke, Pilsen
Designer: Skoda Works
Location: Belgrade Military Museum, Serbia

Barrel length: 10ft
Weight: 23 tons
Caliber: 305mm (12-inch)
Max range: 5.9 miles

Škoda was founded in Plzeň—then in the Austro-Hungarian Empire—in 1859 and was bought by Czech engineer Emil Škoda in 1869, quickly becoming the largest arms manufacturer in the empire. The first big mortar, the 240mm M98 proved to have too short a range and poor ammunition. Development of the Model 1911 (M11) mortar began in 1906, firing first in 1910 when it was seen that the special 847lb armor-piercing shells could penetrate around six feet of reinforced concrete.

In the end there were three versions. The original, the improved M11/16 on a mounting with the capability to travers 360 degrees, and the M16 with a longer barrel improving the range to range 13,500yd. The mortar was transported in three sections (barrel/carriage/platform) by a bespoke M12 100hp 15-ton Austro-Daimler road tractor and trailer. With a crew of 15–17, it could be assembled and readied to fire in around fifty minutes and could fire ten to twelve rounds an hour.

The Austro-Hungarian Ministry of War ordered twenty-four M11s, the total manufactured rising to around eighty which after the war went on to equip the armies of Yugoslavia, Romania, Italy, Czechoslovakia, and Hungary. In 1939, after the Anchluss, Germany took all the available mortars from Czechoslovakia and then all from Yugoslavia. They were designated 30.5cm Mörser (t) or (j).The German Army used eight at the start of the war on the Western Front to help destroy destroy the Belgian fortresses around Liege, Namur, and Antwerp before all the weapons were moved to the eastern and southern fronts. In World War II they equipped German Heavy Artillery Battalions 624, 641, and 815 and Heavy Static Artillery Batteries 230 and 779.

Below: *Škoda M11 Mörser on the Italian front.*

Below: *Austro-Hungarian 305mm siege mortar/howitzer being towed by a motor tractor, together with its complete crew.*

This Page: *Side view of the M11 in Belgrade Military Museum, Serbia.*

1912: French Navy 340mm Modèle 1912 Gun

340MM MODEL 1912

20th Century
France
Maker: Fonderie de Ruelle
Location: None extant

Length: 52ft 10.5in
Weight: 65. 9 tons
Caliber: 340mm
(13.4 inches)
Max range: 7.4 miles at 47.5 degrees with a 1,268lb shell

Compared to the British and German navies, the French Navy built relatively few dreadnoughts (only the four "Courbet" class laid down in 1911) and only three "Bretagne" class superdreadnoughts completed in 1915/16. The former were armed with the ubiquitous 305mm/12-inch gun but the latter carried ten 340mm (13.4-inch) guns in five twin turrets. These guns weighed sixty-six tons and fired a 1,224lb AP shell to a range of only 15,860 yards due to the fact that the twin mounting restricted elevation to twelve degrees. When these ship were modernized between the wars the mountings were modified to allow twenty-three degrees of elevation which increased effective range to 29,090 yards. In all cases the 338lb propellant charge was in four separate bags and rate of fire was a respectable two rounds per minute.

The 340mm M1912 gun was also intended for the "Normandie" class battleships laid down in 1913/14 but never completed. These ships would have mounted twelve guns in three quadruple turrets and subsequently the guns were stored before being used in coastal batteries at Toulon and Quiberon in World War II. In addition the battleship *Lorraine* was scuttled at Toulon in November 1942 and the Germans removed her two after twin turrets which were then installed as coastal batteries. Bizarrely they ended up being engaged by sister ship *Lorraine* during the allied invasion of Southern France in August 1944.

Many of these 340mm guns were available for use as railway guns. The US Army's 53rd Coast Artillery had two batteries of them. Most of the French railway guns were taken and used by the German army in World War II.

Left: *Sister ship* Provence *was scuttled at Toulon in November 1942 following the German occupation of Vichy France. Subsequently the Germans salvaged two of the main armament gun turrets and installed them ashore as coast defense artillery near Toulon, one of which is shown here.*

This Page: *The heaviest French naval gun used in World War I was the 340mm/13.4-inch which armed the three "Provence" class battleships completed in 1915/16. These carried ten such guns in five twin mountings, two each fore and aft (A, B, X and Y), and one amidships (Q). This is* Lorraine *with Q turret clearly visible although it was removed in the 1930s to make space for an aircraft hanger and catapults.*

13.5-INCH MK. V GUN

20th Century
Great Britain
Maker: Vickers
Location: none extant

Barrel length: 50in 6in
Weight: c. 75 tons
Caliber: 13.5 inches
Max range: c. 23 miles

1912: Royal Navy 13.5-inch/45-cal Mk. V Gun

A 13.5-inch 67.5-ton gun had been developed in the 1880s and armed several pre-dreadnoughts but had been abandoned in favor of the lighter and faster firing 12-inch gun. However, the subsequent build up of the German Navy with new well-armored ships made the case for heavier caliber shells with greater armor penetration characteristics. For shells fired at the same muzzle velocity (typically around 2,600ft/sec) the momentum of a heavier shell means that it is less affected by air resistance so that it is travelling much faster when it hits a target. As its kinetic energy is proportional to the square of velocity, as well as in proportion to increased mass, the overall effect is significantly greater than consideration of the small increase in caliber would appear to indicate. Commencing with the "Orion" class laid down in 1909 the 13.5-inch gun was adopted and these "superdreadnoughts" carried ten guns in five twin turrets all mounted on the centerline. The Mk. V gun was a new design unrelated to the earlier weapon and initially fired a 1,250lb shell to a range of 23,800yd at twenty degrees' elevation. However once in service these proved to be excellent weapons with good accuracy and very low barrel wear. Consequently it was decided to adopt a heavier 1,400lb projectile with range being maintained by slightly increasing the propellant charge from 293lb to 297lb, this version then being designated Mk. V(H) and the earlier versions becoming the Mk. V(L).

These guns equipped twelve Royal Navy battleships and four battlecruisers. In addition in 1914 Britain requisitioned the almost complete battleship *Rashadeih* then under construction for the Turkish Navy. Renamed HMS *Erin* she was armed with Mk. VI 13.5-inch guns which only differed in details of their construction and fired the same shells as the Mk. V although using a slightly reduced charge.

Three of the guns were used as railway guns in World War II.

Left: *HMS* Orion *was the first of a new breed of superdreadnoughts armed with the new 13.5in gun.*

Right: *A quarterdeck view of the HMS* Emperor of India *after 13.5in turrets, an "Iron Duke" class dreadnought launched in 1913.*

1913: Krupp 420mm Gamma Mortar

GAMMA MÖRSER

20th Century
Germany
Manufacturers: Krupp
Location: none extant

Barrel length: 22ft 0.7in
Weight: 154 tons
Caliber: 420mm
Max range: 9 miles

The *Gamma Mörser* (mortar) or *Gamma Gerät* was the third iteration of a fort-busting supergun built by Krupp on the eve of World War I. It was designed after promptings by the Fortress Department of the German General Staff at the same time as the *M-Gerät* howitzer "Big Bertha." In fact the two guns are often confused and both were built as a result of a compromise between their different modes of road and rail mobility. The huge Gamma mortar entered service in 1913 and was used in the successful reduction of the Belgian defenses at Liege and other of the during the first German offensive in 1914 and later at Verdun in 1916. With a rifled steel barrel breech-loading Gamma fired a high explosive shell of 1,953lb to a range of nine miles. It used a hydro-pneumatic recoil system and separate case charges. It was transported in ten loads exclusively by rail and assembled mounted on a concrete platform, with an optional armored gunhouse for crew protection. The *Bettungsgeschütz*, or "bedding gun" concrete platform method was a tactical limitation since it was required to be made on site and took a week to complete before the gun could be reassembled.

Some ten Gammas were built in total and one survived beyond the war to resurface later under Hitler's Nazi regime when it was recommissioned and used against the Maginot Line in France and at the siege of Sebastapol in Russia.

Right: *The huge 420mm mortar in position in front of Liège, August 1914. A second is visible in the background.*

1914: Krupp 420mm Typ M-Gerät 14 Howitzer

On the eve of World War I the Germans were well ahead of the allies when it came to superheavy guns, having taken note of the Japanese use of heavy artillery in the war against Russia. With the encouragement of the government, Krupp came up with the largest artillery piece in the world to date—the mobile 420mm (16.5-inch) M-Gerät howitzer, better known as "Big Bertha." A pair of them was produced secretly and they were ready just in time for the start of hostilities, when they were used successfully against the Belgian forts at Liege, Namur, and Antwerp, in conjunction with the 420mm Gamma mortar. They were also used to reduce some Russian defenses. However, when it came to the French forts at Verdun built with reinforced steel they couldn't penetrate them fully and so were gradually phased out, superseded by other heavier weapons. Twelve were built in all, some burst their barrels due to faulty ammunition.

Late in the war some "Berthas" were modified with a smaller L/30 305mm (12-inch) barrel to provide longer-range, lighter fire. Two Berthas were captured by the US and taken home for display before being eventually scrapped.

"Big Bertha" fired an explosive shell weighing 1,807lb to a range of 7.8 miles at a rate of eight rounds an hour. It took a crew of almost 300 men to transport and operate, being driven into action disassembled on five custom-made wagons hauled by motor tractors and included a massive spade-shaped wedge that was buried in the ground to help anchor the weapon. For long-distance transportation the whole set-up was entrained. Reassembly took around six hours.

Below: *One of the prototypes of "Big Bertha." It's possible that the name is linked Gustav Krupp's wife, Bertha. While they performed well in 1914—Fort Loncon was catastrophically demolished inside two hours—by 1916 they were decommissioned after the Battle of Verdun when allied artillery of longer range was introduced.*

1914: Škoda 420mm M14/16 Howitzer

420MM M14/16 HOWITZER

20th Century
Czechoslovakia
Manufacturer: Škoda
Location: National Military Museum, Bucharest, Romania

Barrel length: 20ft 8in
Weight: 116 tons
Caliber: 420mm
Max range: 16,000yd

As well as the 240mm and 305mm mortars/howitzers (see pages 112–113), Škoda designed and built small numbers of a variety of superheavy artillery pieces for use in World War I. The 240mm M16 siege howitzer was designed as a longer-range weapon than the mortars/howitzers. To speed production it used the same carriage and firing platform as the 380mm howitzer, which was an upgrade of the 305mm M16 mortar.

The 420mm L/15 Coastal Howitzer (*Küstenhaubitze*) M14 was designed for port protection in a circular mounting with 360-degree traverse (see photos below). However, demand for heavy artillery on land led to the decision to make them mobile. Škoda worked on an improvised carriage and the first mobile version saw action at Tarnow in Poland in 1915.

In 1916, there was a redesign that included a simple base box, similar to that used by the 305mm mortar and 380mm howitzer. Designated the *Autohaubitze* (meaning it could be towed by automobile) M16, it could be divided into six pieces and towed by M12 or M17 heavy tractors. However, towing the gun was only part of the problem. A battery of one gun, included of 210 men, 8 officers, 5 horses, 4 carts and 32 trucks and took between twelve and forty hours to set the piece up.

There was a subsequent improvement that reduced the size of base-box, reducing weight, and cutting down the number of tractors to four. While this M17 version didn't see action in World War I, one was used in World War II by the Germans against the Maginot Line and during the siege of Sebastopol.

Opposite: *The Škoda M16 380mm siege howitzer in the Army Museum in Vienna. Two were delivered in time to fight in World War I. Another,* Gudrun *is in Bucharest museum.*

Right and Far Right: *The Skoda 420mm M14/16 coastal howitzer was designed to be used from a static position, and the first made was already in position and tested before it was decided to use them in a mobile form.*

1914: US Navy 14-inch Guns

14-INCH GUN

20th Century
United States
Maker: US Naval Gun Factory/Bethlehem Steel
Designer: Bureau of Ordnance
Location: USS *Texas*, near Houston, TX
Barrel length: 52ft 6in
Weight: 71.25 tons (Mk. 1)
Caliber: 14 inches (356mm)
Max range: 34,300 yd (modernized turret

Like most of the European navies the US Navy's first series of dreadnoughts were armed with 12-inch guns but in response to the Royal Navy moving up to a 13.5-inch caliber it decided to go one better and introduced 14-inch gun in the "New York" class laid down in 1911. These ships carried ten 14-inch/45-cal guns in five twin turrets and the same gun armed the subsequent "Oklahoma" class which also carried ten guns but arranged in two twin and two triple mountings. Weighing 62 tons each and firing a 1,500lb shell, the guns in the "New York" class could only elevate to fifteen degrees to give a range of 23,000yd but this increased in later ships to 34,300yd from mountings which could elevate to thirty degrees. Similar guns were mounted in the "Pennsylvania" (1912/13) class which carried twelve 14-inch guns in four triple turrets, a configuration which then was repeated in the "New Mexico" (1914) and "Tennessee" (1915) classes although these mounted the new 14-inch/50-cal gun when they were completed between 1918 and 1920. In addition each gun could be elevated independently as opposed to the common cradle used in the earlier triple mountings. Variously designated Mk. 7 or Mk. 11 and weighing 80 tons, the 50-cal gun fired the same 1,500lb shell to a range of 36,300 yards at thirty degrees' elevation

Interestingly American 14-inch/45-cal guns were carried by four British monitors completed in 1915. These guns were originally intended for the Greek battlecruiser *Salamis* which was under construction in Germany but when war broke out the British naval blockade prevented their delivery. The manufacturer, Bethlehem Steel, offered them to the British Admiralty who then designed the "Abercrombie" class shallow draft monitors around these weapons, each ship carrying one twin mounting. It is also worth noting that Britain produced a 14-inch/45-cal gun to arm the Chilean battleship *Almirante Latorre* which was purchased by the Admiralty in 1914 and renamed HMS *Canada*. After the war she was sold back to Chile in 1920 and subsequently survived until 1959 when she was scrapped.

Left: *As completed the USS* Texas *carried a total of ten guns in five twin turrets, two forward as shown here, one immediately abaft the funnels at main deck level, and two on the quarterdeck with X turret superfiring over Y turret.*

This Page: *USS* Texas *(BB35) was the first US battleship to be armed with 14-inch guns as were all subsequent battleships completed for the US Navy during World War I. Today the ship is preserved as a memorial museum at Galveston, Texas.*

1914: Canon de 274mm Modèle 1893/96 Railroad Gun

Below: *A 274 mm Schneider Model 1893/1896 gun on a sliding railway carriage, World War I.*

With France caught short of heavy artillery at the start of World War 1 a solution was found in the modification of heavy naval guns originally designed for battleships that had been canceled. Many of these were put onto railroad mountings to provide a mobility that early internal combustion engines or steam tractors couldn't. The heyday of the railway gun, many of the World War I units would go on to be used in World War II. The *Canon de 274 mm Modèle 1893/96* guns had been designed for use by the French Navy (274mm/40 (10.4-inch as on *Henri IV*) Model 1893/1896 and surplus guns were provided sliding-carriage mountings by Schneider et Cie (manufacturers of the first French tank, the Schneider CA1). These mountings had minimal traverse and had to be fired from a curved track. After 500 shots the barrels were bored out to 285mm.

Below: *The precursor of the railway guns of World War I and II, this 32-pdr Brooke naval rifle was used by Robert E. Lee's forces at the siege of Petersburg in the American Civil War.*

This Page: *A 274mm/45 Model 1887/1893 railroad gun captured by US troops near Rentwertshausen, Thuringia, Germany, on April 10, 1945. Originally the French naval 10.8-inch guns equipped pre-dreadnought battleships but were transferred to railroad guns by the French. Captured by the German Army when France fell in 1940 they were used throughout World War II.*

CANON DE 274MM RAILROAD GUN

20th Century
France
Location: None extant

Barrel length: 37ft 8in
Weight: 11.5 tons
Caliber: 274mm
(10.8 inches)
Max range: c. 16 miles

1915: Canon de 305mm 1893/96 Railroad Gun

CANON DE 305MM 1893/96

19th Century
France
Maker: Fonderie de Ruelle
Location: None extant

Barrel length: 40 feet
Weight: 53 tons
Caliber: 305mm (12 inches)
Max range: 7.3 miles

The French Canon de 305mm Modèle 1893/96 had equipped a number of French battleship classes—the "Charlemagne," "République," and "Liberté" classes—as well as the one-off *Iéna* and *Suffren*. It became one of the naval weapon sthat was converted for use as a railway gun. The 12-inch guns were fitted onto both rotating center-pintle (Saint-Chamond) and sliding (Schneider) carriages. Unlike the naval mounting which could only fire its 769lb shells up to a range of 13,000yd, the railway version could achieve an elevation of 40 degrees giving a much improved range—out to 34,000 yards, or nearly twenty miles. At the end of the war, the old barrels were rebored to 320mm becoming the 320mm modèle 1917.

By the end of hostilities the French had more than 400 railway guns of different calibers. These new railroad weapons were seen as the best way of fielding superlarge guns and all the main states involved in the war produced them. (See also pp. 132–133.)

Above Right: *France, c. 1917. Canadian Army officers inspecting a Canon de 305mm armed French railroad gun on a center-pintle chassis mount.*

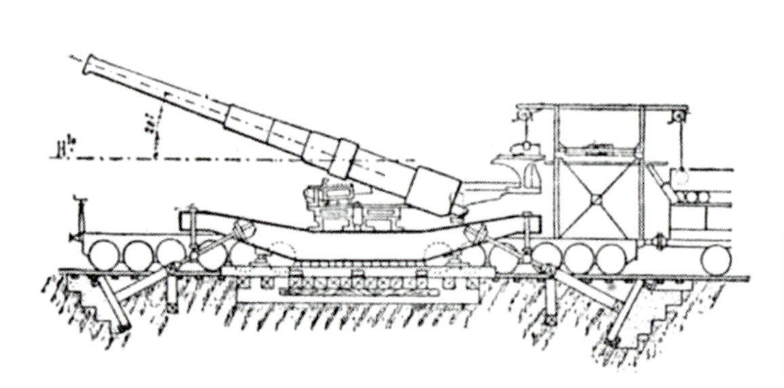

Below Right and Far Right: *The sliding-mount 305mm railway guns.*

Opposite: *The FNS* Jena *a one-off battleship whose main armament was two turrets each with two 305mm M1893/96 guns.*

1915: Royal Navy 15-inch Mk. I Gun

While the Royal Navy standardized on the 13.5-inch gun, some foreign navies including those of the USA and Japan went for the heavier 14-inch gun which fired a slightly larger shell to a similar range. In order to remain one step ahead, and to maintain material superiority over German ships, the Admiralty specified a 15-inch gun for the new "Queen Elizabeth" battleships ordered in 1912. The new gun was basically a scaled up 13.5-inch gun and fired a 1,938lb shell over a range of 26,650yd at twenty degrees' elevation and in the Mk. I twin mounting it was capable of firing two rounds per minute—very creditable for a heavy caliber gun. The twin 15-inch mounting was widely adopted and as well as the "Queen Elizabeth" class it was also carried by the five "R" class battleships, five battlecruisers (*Renown*, *Repulse* and, *Hood*, *Courageous*, *Glorious*) as well as several monitors. Even at the end of World War II the new battleship HMS *Vanguard* was armed with eight 15-inch guns in twin mountings which had been removed from *Courageous* and *Glorious* when they were converted to aircraft carriers. Between the wars four of the "Queen Elizabeth" class and some other ships had their mountings modified to allow thirty degrees of elevation. Designated Mk. I/N, these increased maximum range initially to 29,000yd and later to 32,000yd by the use of more streamlined projectiles. The effectiveness of these changes was dramatically illustrated when HMS *Warspite* achieved a hit on the Italian battleship *Guilio Cesare* at a distance of 26,000yd during the action off Calabria in July 1940—at the time the longest range hit obtained in a moving ship by a naval gun (but see item on German 11-inch gun in Chapter 4).

15-INCH MK. 1 GUN

20th Century
Great Britain
Maker: Vickers
Location: Two guns, from HMS Ramillies and Resolution, but later moved to HMS Roberts, Imperial War Museum in London, England.

Length: 54ft 2.5in
Weight: 100 tons
Caliber: 15 inches (381mm)
Max range: 15 miles

Left: *The forward 15-inch guns of HMS* Repulse, *one of a pair of powerful battlecruisers completed in mid 1916 and just too late to participate in the Battle of Jutland.*

Below: *The five battleships of the "Queen Elizabeth" class commissioned in 1915/16 and were armed with eight 15-inch guns, making them the world's most powerful battleships at that time. The disposition of the guns in paired turrets fore and aft is shown in the World War II image of HMS* Queen Elizabeth.

1916: German Navy 380mm/45-cal SK Gun

380MM SK GUN

20th Century
Germany
Maker: Krupp
Location: No gun, but the Battery Pommern platform survives

Barrel length: 4ft 5in
Weight: 263 tons
Caliber: 380mm (15 inches)
Max range: 14.4 miles

The German Navy always lagged behind the Royal Navy in terms of the number of ships completed and in the caliber of their main armament. Virtually all of their dreadnoughts and battlecruisers were armed with 280mm/11-inch or 305mm/12-inch guns although a 350mm gun (equivalent to the British 13.5-inch) was produced for the "Mackensen" class battlecruisers which were never completed. Belatedly four "Bayern" class battleships were laid down in 1913/14 but only two (*Baden* and *Bayern*) were completed in 1916 and neither was present at the battle of Jutland. Armed with eight 38cm SK L/45 guns, these ships were similar in concept to the British "Queen Elizabeth" class and, although heavily armored, they were 2–3 knots slower.

The gun itself weighed in at seventy-six tons and fired a 1,653lb AP shell to a range of 22,000yd at a sixteen-degree elevation (a slightly shorter distance than the standard German 12-inch SK L/50) but increased to 25,370yd at a twenty-degree elevation. The two elevation figures relate to the maximum elevation available in mountings aboard *Baden* and *Bayern* respectively. The propellant charge was in two parts, the first to be loaded was a bagged 192lb charge and unusually the second 212lb charge was contained in a brass case which in turn permitted a simpler and lighter breech mechanism. This feature enable a higher rate of fire than the British 15-inch guns—almost 2.5 round per minute as against just under two per minute in the "Queen Elizabeth" class. This gun would also have armed the "Ersatz Yorck" class battlecruisers ordered in 1916, none of which were ever completed.

When the construction of further capital ships was suspended many of these guns were diverted for land use and equipped the *Deutschland* and *Pommern* batteries in Belgium from 1917.

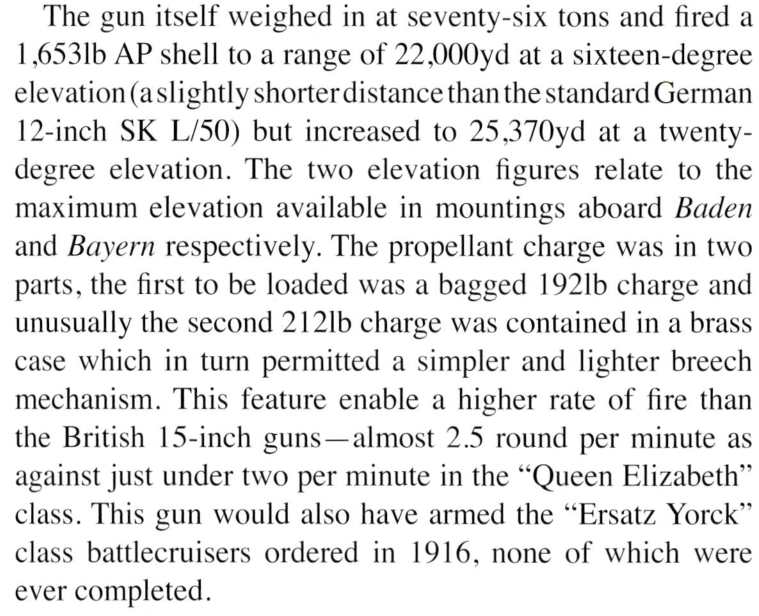

Left: *"Long Max" in Battery* Pommern, *in the Leugenboom district of Koekelare, was one of the biggest guns of the world in 1917. Powerful enough to bombard Dunkirk—some 30 miles away—and Ypres.*

Right: *During World War I only two German battleships armed with 380mm (15-inch) guns were completed. These were SMS* Baden *and SMS* Bayern *of which the former is shown here with identification marks on B (Bruno) and C (Caesar) turrets.*

1916: Obukhovskii 12-inch Naval and Railway Gun

The Obukhov State Plant (1922–1992 it was called the Bolshevik Plant no. 232) was set up in the 19th century to build naval guns. The Obukhovskii 12-inch (300mm) 52-cal Pattern 1907 gun was designed 1906–1907 after the Russo-Japanese War and produced the most powerful gun mounted aboard completed warships of the Imperial Russian and Soviet navies. They proved to be extremely accurate and long-lived, serving through both world wars not just as naval guns (four triple MK-3-12 turrets on the "Gangut" and "Imperatritsa Mariya" classes) but as coastal artillery (in the Peter the Great Naval Fortress and along the Tallinn-Porkkala defensive line, and as turreted batteries around the Baltic Sea, Sebastopol, and Vladivostok) and as a railway gun during World War II. The guns of the *Imperator Alexandr III* (*Volya*—Freedom—to the Soviets) ended up in the Nazi Batterie Mirius on Guernsey in the Channel Islands. Naval orders reached 198 guns and around 150 were delivered by the end of 1917. Fourteen others were finished in 1921 and a few others were later completed.

Imperatritsa Mariya was lost at Sebastopol in 1916 after a magazine exploded. She was raised but eventually scrapped in 1926. Her gun turrets were also raised. Three of them were used for TM-3-12 railway guns and saw action in the Soviet-Finnish war in 1939–1940. Two went to 30th Coast Defense Battery, Sebastopol where they were put out of action during the German siege.

Below: *The rail gun version of the Obukhovskii 12-incher was the TM-3-12.*

OBUKHOVSKII 12-INCH GUN

20th Century
Soviet Union
Maker: Leningradsky Metallichesky
Designer: Obukhov State Plant
Location: 1938 Railway gun TM-3-12 at Victory Park, Moscow, Russia

Barrel length: 47ft
Weight: 56 tons
Caliber: 12 inches (305mm)
Max range: 19 miles
Max range: 13,000 yards

Right: *The guns were mounted in triple turrets. This is the Soviet battleship* Parizhskaia Kommuna, *which had been laid down as the Tsarist* Sevastopol. *She fought at Sebastopol and survived the war ending up as a training ship until decommissioned in 1956.*

Right: *The largest guns to be emplaced on the Channel Islands, Batterie Mirus boasted four 30.5cm guns from the* Imperator Aleksandr III. *After serving briefly in the Tsarist Navy in 1917,* Imperator Alexandr III *was apropriated by the Soviets in 1917, captured by the Germans at Sebastopol in 1918, passed to the British after the German surrender the same year, taken on by the White Russians as* General Alekseyev *at Izmir in 1919, she was interned by the French when the Russians were defeated. The French sent the guns to Finland and Norway at the start of World War II and four were captured by the Germans. They were sent to Guernsey as part of the Atlantic Wall, they were scrapped after the war.*

Opposite: *305mm twin coastal artillery turret in Kuivasaari Coastal Artillery Fortress. This turret was constructed by Finns 1931–1934 by using guns from Ino fortress and a 356mm (14-inch) twin turret barbette. When the Finns declared independence a number of Obukhov 305mm guns were taken; in January 1940 France gave the Finns twelve more—of which four were captured by the Germans (see above). Two of the barrels were used to build two single gun turrets on Isosaari Island to beef up the defenses of Helsinki; two further barrels were used for a new dual gun turret on Mäkiluoto; three more were used to repair Soviet TM-3-12 railroad guns abandoned at Hanko when the Soviets evacuated in 1941; one was kept at a spare.* Info from www.alternativefinland.com/kuivasaari-coastal-artillery-fortress.

Opposite, Inset: *Breech of Kuivasaari 305 mm gun. This is the left gun of a twin turret. The inscription on the barrel says: "Obukhovskiy Steleliteyniy Zavod [Obukhovskiy Steel Plant in St.Petersburg], 1911, S.A. [land artillery], N 105, 52 K [length of barrel in calibers]."*

German Railroad Guns

388MM SK L/45

20th Century
Germany
Manufacturers: Krupp
Location: Pommern Battery

Length: 103ft 10in
Barrel length: 53ft
Weight: 267.9 tons
Caliber: 380mm
Max range: 60,000 yards

1915: 380mm SK L/45 "Max"

By 1915, Professor Fritz Rausenberger, Krupp's chief ordnance technician, had successfully mated several modified naval guns with railroad mountings to develop a series of long-range railroad guns. The 380mm (15-inch) SK L/45 "Max" (aka Langer Max) railway gun employed the most powerful German naval gun of World War I, equipping the "Baden," "Bayern," and "Ersatz Yorck" class battleships. The guns that would have equipped two of the class "Bayern" class, the *Sachsen* and *Württemberg* went to equip two coastal batteries *Pommern* and *Deutschland* (see page 133) and another to form the basis of the Paris Gun (see page 144).

With a horizontal sliding-block breech and hydro-pneumatic recoil, "Max" fired both HE and shrapnel shells weighing up to 1,650lb to a range of 60,000yd. Like the Paris Gun it was at first transported by rail to a custom-made concrete emplacement where it was assembled and used with a full traverse of 360 degrees. However, this method was found to take too long, so Krupp modified the "Max" guns to fit and fire on their own railway chassis trucks; traverse now became a question of custom-made curved rails and recoil relied on both cradle and back-rolling systems. The gun had to be reloaded at zero elevation and needed reaiming for each shot. "Max" first saw use in fixed position emplacements during the battle of Verdun and-later complete railway versions fought in 1918's final battles including the second battle of the Marne. Eight guns were built in total, one was abandoned in Belgium during the retreat and later sold by the Belgians to the French, the others made it back to Germany but were destroyed after the war by the victorious Allies.

1916: 210mm SK L/40 and SK L/45 "Peter Adalbert"

Krupp designed and built eleven of the 210mm (8.3-inch) SK L/40 and SK L/45 "Peter Adalbert" superguns, once again made by modifying surplus naval guns. Again like the "Max" guns the "Peter Adalberts" originally fired from a prepared emplacement having been transported by train but some were converted to stay on the rails for quicker use. The SK L/40 weighed 121.74 tons), the SK L/45 weighed 115.37 tons. Both guns had an overall length of 52ft; the L/40 a 27.7ft barrel and the L/46 a 31ft. They fired shells between 250lb and 254lb in weight. They were first used in the Battle of Verdun, but also saw action at the Somme, Passchendaele, Gallipoli, and during the final offensive and battles of 1918. Two guns were destroyed at the end of the war and the rest were assigned to coastal defense.

Right: *The "Scharnhorst" class's main armament was eight 210mm SK L/40 and twenty-one of the spare guns were passed to the army. One went to a coastal unit at Cape Helles in Turkey; seven others became the 210mm SK "Peter Adalbert" railway guns. These were reemployed as coastal artillery during World War II.*

1916: 240mm SK L/40 "Theodor Karl"

Another railway supergun originating from a naval weapon, Krupp produced the 240mm (9.5-inch) SK L/40 "Theodor Karl" type in 1916–1917. They, too, initially required the building of a specific firing emplacement but were then modified to remain on a carriage as a true railway gun, with limited traverse coming from a front pintle mount and rear rollers. Weighing 128.9 tons with a barrel length of 29ft the "Theodor Karls" fired armor-piercing and high-explosive shells of 333lb to a range of 22,000–29,100yd. Over thirty were built, some used for coastal defense and others for use on the Western Front seeing action at the Somme in October 1916. Most were destroyed by the Allies after the war but four were left in their coastal defense positions.

1918: 280mm K L/40 "Kurfürst"

Another in the long line of German surplus naval guns modified into railway guns by Krupp, the 1918 28cm (11-inch) K L/40 "Kurfürst" operated initially with railroad and firing platform before being further modified with a cradle firing system that kept the gun on its carriage, partly bolted down and partly jacked up for the addition of a portable firing platform that increased the traverse from four to 180 degrees. The "Kurfürst" weighed 164 tons with a length of 70ft 11in and a barrel of 34ft L/40. It fired high explosive shells to a range of 19,800–28,300yd. Six were built in total and all saw action on the Western Front, before being destroyed postwar according to the terms of the Versailles Treaty.

Below: *One of four "Theodor Karls" on a railroad mount.*

1918: 240mm SK L/30 "Theodor Otto"

Another modified naval gun constructed by Krupp, the "Theodor Ottos" were mounted onto two four-axle customized railway trucks, with a front pintle and back rollers allowing a small four degrees of traverse when not using rail curvature. The "Theodor Otto" weighed 114 tons with an overall length of 52ft and a barrel of 23ft 5in L/30. It fired several different shells with weights between 309lb and 333lb to a range of maximum firing range of 20,500yd. Four were built and saw service in 1918 on the Western Front with one being captured by US troops.

Right: *SMS* Kaiser Barbarossa *of the "Kaiser Friedrich III" class was armed with a main battery of four 240mm guns. When that and the "Wittelsbach" class battleships were decommissioned the guns were converted to coastal artillery. Eight guns in four turrets were emplaced at Libau; four guns were emplaced at Battery Hamburg on Norderney, and later moved during the war to Cherbourg; four more on Sylt. The remaining twenty-one guns were transferred to the army, a number being converted to railway guns.*

280MM SK L/40 "BRUNO"

20th Century
Germany
Maker: Krupp
Location: Australian War Memorial, Canberra, Australia

Length: 17ft 4in
Weight: 172 tons
Caliber: 283mm (11.14in)
Max range: 18.3 miles

1917: German 280mm SK "Bruno" Railroad Gun

The 280mm SK L/40 "Bruno" was another modified naval gun produced by Krupp from 1917 onwards, first as a rail-ported weapon and then later with the guns remounted as genuine railway guns. The guns came from the "Braunschweig" and "Deutschland" class battleships which had been shown to be obsolete at the battle of Jutland. Some of the guns were used for coastal defense, four on the Friesan island of Wangerooge in Batterie Graf Spee (they would end up in Brest in World War II). About twenty were used as railway guns—mainly for coast defense, protecting the occupied ports of Ostend and Zeebrugge, but only two went to the army; one of them was captured by Australians and now resides in Canberra. After the war some were destroyed and some given to other countries such as Belgium in reparations. Two ended up in protecting the Gironde during World War II.

Right: *Artist William Redver Stark's "Longueau: German Gun Captured on Somme, Aug. 1918, British Drive."*

Opposite: *The "Amiens Gun" captured by Australian soldiers in 1918 on display at the Australian War Memorial in 2009. "Bruno" fired HE shells with a ballistic cap weighing 626lb and a warhead of 50lb TNT to a range of 30,350yd.*

OBUSIER DE 520 MODÈLE 1916

20th Century
France
Maker: Schneider
Location: none extant

Barrel Length: 39ft
Weight: 290 tons
Caliber: 520mm (20 inches)
Max range: 10.5 miles

French Railroad Guns

In Europe the French originally led the field in railway gun development, improvising some for use during the Siege of Paris (1870–1871). In the late 1880s the French arms manufacturer Schneider produced various models including a 4.7-inch (120mm) version mounted on rail carriages. However, by the start of the war France had an acute shortage of heavy artillery. We have already seen 340mm Modèle 1912 naval gun that was used on a rail platform (see p. 114); the *Canon de 274mm Mle 1893/96* (pp. 124–125); and the *Canon de 305mm Mle 1893/96* gun (pp. 126–127). Other French railway guns that need a mention are another 340mm—the Mle 1893; the *Mortier de 370mm Mle 1887*; the *Mortier de 320mm Mle 1870/93* which was used from 1914 until the end of the war and scrapped in 1920; the Obusier de 400mm Mle 15/16—eight were ordered from Saint-Chamond in 1915. They reworked 340mm Mle 1887 naval guns from *Brennus*, *Jemmappes*, and *Valmy*.

Two giant *Obusier de 520* railway howitzers were commissioned by the ALVF (*l'Artillerie Lourds sur Voie Ferrée*) Committee from Schneider in 1916—a French version of "Big Bertha." Due to development delays only one weapon had been delivered by 1917 and this exploded during trials. The surviving gun was not delivered till 1918 and saw no action in the remainder of the war, but was later captured by the Germans at its store at le Cruesot (Schneider's works) in 1940 early in World War II. They used it in the siege of Leningrad, where after a few months use it was also destroyed by a premature shell explosion in its barrel.

The *Obusier de 520* had a rifled L/15 barrel. It was a breech-loader using a combination of cradle and sliding recoil systems. It required bracing when firing its 3,020–3,646lb shells up to a range of 16,000–18,600yd. It was built across two eight-axle railways trucks and had no traverse, being limited to positional traversing through track curvature. It was electrically powered and was accompanied by a generator car.

Below: *French 320mm at the moment of firing.*

Opposite, Right: *The 400mm Mle 15 or 16.*

Below: *An April 1917 photograph of a French 320mm railway gun during World War I. Using guns from the fortresses at Brest and Cherbourg and Schneider sliding mounts, these guns had a rate of fire of one round every five minutes and a range of about twenty miles.*

1918: Royal Navy 18-inch/40-cal Mk. I Gun

This was the largest caliber gun ever to be used by the Royal Navy and was originally intended to arm the light battlecruiser HMS *Furious* which would have carried two 18-inch guns in single mountings fore and aft. The other two ships in the class (*Courageous* and *Glorious*) were armed with two twin 15-inch mountings as already described. *Furious* was laid down on June 8, 1915, at which point three guns had been ordered from Armstrong's Elswick works. Launched in August 1916 she was completed on 26 June 1917 although by then her design had been altered by the removal of the forward 18-inch gun to allow the construction of a flight deck over the forecastle. Although the after gun was initially fitted, it was removed in the following September to allow construction of an after aircraft landing deck.

At that time the Royal Navy maintained a flotilla of shallow-draft monitors equipped with 12-inch, 14-inch and 15-inch guns off the Belgium coast but these were regularly outranged by German shore batteries so it was proposed that the now surplus 18-inch guns be mounted on these ships. As the guns were too big to fit the standard mountings they were carried aft on fixed land mountings permanently trained to starboard, capable of only limited traverse (twenty degrees) and housed under a large angular gunshield. In the event only the monitors *General Wolfe* and *Lord Clive* were fitted out and saw some action in the closing months of the war. During this time *Wolfe* opened fire at German positions just south of Ostend at a range of 36,000yd—the longest range ever fired in action by the Royal Navy.

The Mk. I gun itself weighed 149 tons and fired a massive 3,320lb projectile. As mounted on HMS *Furious* it could achieve a range of 28,800yd but the monitor mountings allowed up to forty-five degrees of elevation to give 36,000yd (40,100yd with supercharges). All three guns were scrapped between the wars and work on an 18-inch/45-cal weapon was canceled in 1922 as a result of the Washington Treaty (see Chapter 4).

Below: James Wolfe *built by Palmers, Newcastle launched September 1915 Served in the Dover Monitor Squadron. Originally two BL 12-inch Mk. VIIIs in a single turret, two QF 3-pdr guns.* Lord Clive *and* General Wolfe *had an additional single BL 18-inch Mk. I in 1918 installed aft. Broken up in 1921.*

Right: *The light battlecruiser HMS* Furious *was intended to be armed with two single 18in guns but in the event only the after mounting was installed as shown here. The forward gun was deleted so that an aircraft flying-off deck could be constructed.*

18-INCH MK. 1 GUN

20th Century
Great Britain
Maker: Elswick Ordnance Co
Location: none extant

Length: 62ft
Weight: 149 tons
Caliber: 18 inches (457mm)
Max range: 20.4 miles

1918: The Paris Gun—Krupp 210mm Railroad Gun

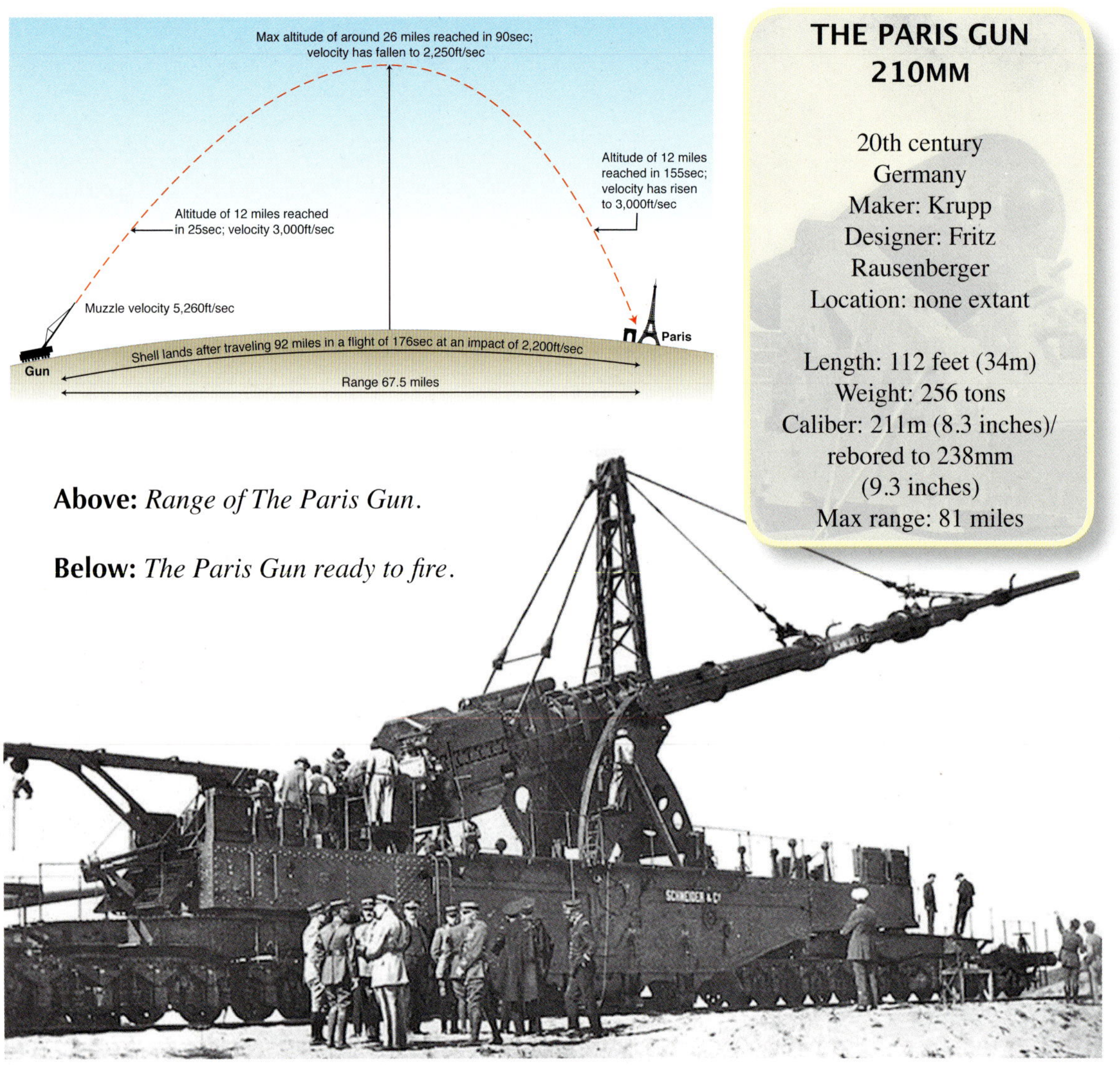

Above: *Range of The Paris Gun.*

Below: *The Paris Gun ready to fire.*

THE PARIS GUN 210MM

20th century
Germany
Maker: Krupp
Designer: Fritz Rausenberger
Location: none extant

Length: 112 feet (34m)
Weight: 256 tons
Caliber: 211m (8.3 inches)/ rebored to 238mm (9.3 inches)
Max range: 81 miles

In 1918 the Germans began shelling the French capital with a colossal supergun known at first as *Kaiser Wilhelm Geschütz* but soon called after its target—the Paris Gun or Pariser Kanone. It fired from so far away it was thought the city was being bombed by a very high altitude Zeppelin airship until shell fragments proved otherwise. The munitions used achieved new records in range and height by traveling over seventy-five miles in under two minutes reaching 24.9 miles) into the stratosphere. Manufactured by Krupp based on a 380mm (15-inch) naval gun fitted with an internal tube reducing the caliber to 210mm (8-inch), the Paris Gun had a barrel length of 112ft—so long that it needed to be braced when firing its 234lb shells to a range of eighty-one miles in under two minutes. The wear and tear on the barrel of these monster munitions was so great that they necessitated reboring after relatively few shots, spare barrels and the use of progressively larger caliber ammunition to compensate for the erosion. It was operated by the German navy with a crew of eighty and was mounted on a railway carriage chassis for rail transport although fired from a custom built concrete emplacement. In all seven Paris guns were made although lacking enough special carriages they were used no more than in pairs. In order to disguise their signature from aerial spotters they were hidden in a forest near other artillery and though soon spotted none were ever captured or recovered after the German retreat.As a terror weapon it was certainly sensational in its initial impact, achieving the coup of reaching the city from a record range and trajectory, but the Paris Gun lacked a real killer punch.

British Railroad Guns

Britain's first rail gun was sent to South Africa in 1900 during the Boer War. As with other industrialized nations Britain developed its World War I rail guns primarily from surplus naval guns with the 9.2-inch Mk. 3 being heavily used, firing 45,000 rounds during World War I. It could fire a 1,582lb rounds to a range of 34,800yd.

Armstrong's Elswick Ordnance Co. built many of Britain's rail guns, including the 12-inch railway howitzer which saw extensive use on the Western Front from 1916 operated by the Royal Garrison Artillery. By 1918, there were sixty-seven of these in various marks operating and they had expended a total of 277,000 rounds. In particular, the success of the Mk. V saw it remain in service during World War II.

The superheavy BL series including 12-inch, 14-inch and 18-inch guns were all constructed from existing naval breech-loading guns and all were mounted on railway carriages for transport. In 1915 four 12-inchers were built with 40ft barrels firing 850lb HE shells to a range of 32,700 yards using a mixture of sliding and backward rolling recoil systems. Having no traverse the guns were aimed by using the curvature of the custom-built firing tracks. All four saw service on the Western Front.

In 1918 two 14-inch railway guns were built by Elswick Ordnance Co. using Mk. III 14-inch naval guns by with the same recoil and traversing systems as the 12-inch version. They saw very brief service before the war's end and, being an unusual caliber size for British artillery, they were soon obsolete and scrapped in 1926. They weighed 250 tons each, with a barrel length of 52.5ft firing an HE shell weighing 1,586lb with a range of 34,600yd. A shell of 1,586lb introduced later had a range of 28,000 yds When used on the Western Front they were mounted on the *Boche Buster* and the *Scene Shifter* carriages.

BL 14-INCH RAILWAY GUN

20th Century
Great Britain
Maker: Armstrong, Elswick Ordnance Co Location: none extant

Barrel length: 52ft
Weight: 248 tons
Caliber: 14 inches (356mm)
Max range: 21.5 miles

Far Left: *Crew and British BL 18-inch railway howitzer at Ashbury Station prior to firing into Okehampton Artillery Range.*

Left: *The World War II British BL 18-inch howitzer Mk. I mounted on* Boche Buster *(which carried a 14-inch gun in WWI). Seen outside Bourne Park Tunnel near the English South coast.*

1920: Royal Navy BL 18-inch Railroad Howitzer

18-INCH RAILROAD HOWITZER

20th Century
Great Britain
Maker: Armstrong
Location: Royal Armories Museum, Fort Nelson, Hampshire, England

Barrel length: 52ft (34.7m)
Weight: 85.7 tons
Caliber: 18 inches (457mm)
Max range: 12.6 miles

Although developed by Armstrong during World War I along the same lines as the previous BL series, the 18-inch railway howitzer wasn't ready until 1920. It fired HE shells weighing 2,500lb to a range of 22,300yd. Five guns and two carriages were completed for the project but having missed the hostilities they were never fired in anger but put into storage, then used for testing. A single 18-inch barrel survives today at the Royal Armories artillery museum at Fort Nelson in Hampshire.

The carriages for the 18-inch howitzer were later reused in 1940 to mount some 13.5-inch guns for home defense. Originally used for super-dreadnought battleships during World War I, three BL 13.5-inch Mk. Vs were brought out of retirement in 1939 in the early days of World War II to serve as coastal defense artillery in the area of the Dover Straits.

With their range only just reaching the French coast, their role was mainly to harass and interdict enemy shipping. They had a barrel length of 50ft 6in and fired HE and AP shells weighing up to 1,400lb to a range of 23,820yd. When not in use they were hidden in railway tunnels. One experimental high-velocity version was made with an extended liner that projected beyond the barrel firing supercharged smoke shells into the stratosphere for research purposes and was never used for active combat.

Below Left: *BL 18-inch railway howitzer, seen at a temporary exhibition in Spoorwegmuseum, Utrecht, Netherlands.*

Below: *8-inch gun M1888 on carriage M1918 possibly one of three weapons delivered to France in World War I.*

American Railroad Guns

The United States was quick to develop railroad guns, mounting various heavy weapons on carriages during the Civil War. By the time it entered World War I, it had become obvious that the US land forces needed railway guns—all the other combattants had them—so it impressed the M1888 8-inch (203mm) coastal artillery piece into immediate service. Forty-seven were ordered, and but only three made it to France before the Armistice. They did see extensive postwar service, however, with most (sources vary on the numbers) being delivered and along with thirty-two 8-inch Mk. VI railway guns (M3A2) they were used for coast defense. Also modified were some of the 12-inch coast defense mortars, ninety-one of these in total having railway mounts (see pp. 154–155). During World War II, a battery of four of these mortars was used as part of the temporary harbor defenses of Grays Harbor, Washington. The main US railway gun to see action was the 14-inch 50-cal (see next page).

Left: *The 14-inch 50-cal naval gun on the Mk II mount—no armored house for the crew; rolling recoil; more axles (twenty instead of twelve). Note the winch at the front. As the gun recoiled it would move back as much as 40ft and would need to be winched back to its firing position.*

Below: *14-inch 50-caliber US Navy railway gun, seen in 1920.*

1918: US 14-inch/50-cal Railroad Gun

In 1918 the obvious imbalance between the Allies' artillery assets and those of Germany led the US to develop the 14-inch/50-caliber railway gun using the largest naval weapon available at the time for the purpose—the 14-inch/50 Mk. 4. A dozen were modified in two marks, mounted on railway trucks and manned by US Navy crews. Five saw action in France in the closing months of World War I. Each battery had its own locomotive, gun, ammunition, and accommodation cars and traveled as a discrete unit, traverse being achieved mainly through rail curvature (the gun itself had a limited traverse of 2.5 degrees). The main difference between the two marks was in the recoil systems—the first using a very complicated and time-consuming pit and jack method; the second a more conventional spring and roll back system. The 14-inch/50-cal had fired shells weighing 1,400lb to a distance of 42,000yd. They were used to bombard and disrupt German military infrastructure deep behind the front lines. One of the guns can be seen today on display outside the US Navy Museum at the Washington Navy Yard.

Above Left: *Men of the 35th Coast Artillery loading a 14-inch/50 Mk. II railroad gun.*

Left: *US 14-inch railroad gun on Mk. I rail car from World War I, photographed at the Washington Navy Yard.*

14-INCH RAILROAD GUN

20th Century
United States
Maker: Baldwin Locomotive Works
Location: US Navy Museum, Washington Navy Yard, Washington DC, USA

Barrel length: 58ft
Weight: with carriage over 0.5 million pounds
Caliber: 14 inches (356mm)
Max range: 23.8 miles

1920: US 14-inch M1920 Railroad Gun

The 14-inch M1920 was upgrade of the 14-inch/50 designed in 1920 for coastal defense. This fired HE and AP shells to a range of 48,220yd. The main difference between the models was in the railway carriage system, which was adapted to be able to raised and lowered, enabling the guns to be transferred to pre-fixed mounts in coastal fortifications with full 360-degree traverse or used as a fixed railway gun with seven degrees of traverse using rail curvature. Only four guns were produced and went into service between 1925 and 1946. Two were deployed to Fort MacArthur and the other two to forts defending the Panama Canal.

14-INCH M1920 RAILROAD GUN

20th Century
United States
Maker: Watervliet Arsenal
Location: none extant

Barrel length: 59ft 6in
Weight: c. 112 tons
Caliber: 14 inches (356mm)
Max range: 27 miles

Left: *Battery B, 3rd Coast Artillery Regiment firing the M1920 14-inch railroad gun at Fort MacArthur in 1927. It was the last large-caliber railway gun to be deployed by the US Army.*

16-INCH M1919 GUN

19th/20th century
United States
Maker: Watervliet Arsenal
Designer: US Army Ordnance Corps
Location: Aberdeen Proving Ground, MD, USA

Barrel length: 66ft 10in
Weight: 484 tons
Caliber: 16 inches (406mm)
Max range: 27.8 miles

1920: US 16-inch/50-cal M1919 Coastal Gun

The 16-inch (406mm)/50-caliber M1919 was a massive supergun used for coastal defense. The program had its origins in 1895 when a single prototype M1895 was ordered. Completed in 1902, it served in the Panama Canal Zone until scrapped in 1943.

Half a dozen of a second version, the Model 1919, were then built and deployed in coastal defenses around the US including New York, Boston, and Pearl Harbor, Hawaii. These used a barbette carriage system favored by coastal artillery. Weighing 484 tons with a barrel length of 66.8ft the 16-inch/50 fired AP and HE shells weighing up to 2,340lb to a range of 49,100yd.

After the Washington Naval Treaty of 1922 led to the canceling of various naval big gun projects, twenty unused or surplus guns became available leading to Mk. 2 and Mk. 3 version they had been destined for "South Dakota" class battleships and "Lexington" class battlecruisers. These were used in pairs for the defense of Pearl Harbor and San Francisco. The further release in 1940 of some fifty surplus 16-inch/50 guns enabled the beginning of a program to equip new casemated defenses at strategic points along the US coastline. However, in 1943 when the threat of invasion had subsided, the program was terminated with only twenty forts having been built. When the war ended in 1945 the 16-inch/50s began to be scrapped and all had disappeared by 1948.

Right: *Fort Tilden is located in Queens, New York City, and was established in 1917. In 1921 Battery Harris was created to house a pair of M1919 16-inch guns. They were provided with covered emplacement during World War II (as seen here). In 1942–1944 Battery Isaac N. Lewis was built in Highlands NJ, also with two casemated 16-inch/50-caliber Mk. 2 guns.*

Left: *One of two 16-inch gun M1919 on Fort Duvall, Hog Island, Hull, MA. Note the barbette mounting: the guns were casemated in 1942 in case of air attack. Fort Duvall was built in the early 1920s to defend Boston and the surrounding harbor areas. Fire control was from a tall fire control tower at Point Allerton—it's still surviving. The guns and military presence on the island have gone now, the guns scrapped in 1948.*

Right and Opposite, Below Left: *The original M1895 16-inch gun, at Watervliet Arsenal. Still in use, the arsenal is the oldest continuously active arsenal in the United States, having been founded in 1813. The gun weighed 284,000lb—a real heavyweight and at the time the heaviest ever—the railroad carriage used to transport itself weighed 192,420lb.*

Below Right: *This is a Mk. 2 one of only four M1919/50s that have survived and the only Mk. 3 It's at Aberdeen Proving Ground, MD on a test mounting. The Mk. 2 and Mk. 3 guns were supposed to be used in the "Iowa" class battleships, but nobody told the designers! Farcically, the turrets were too small and new guns had to be manufactured. This left the army with an embarrassment of riches and over seventy big guns to house. By war's end twenty-one batteries had been built but not all had been armed. Most of the guns were scrapped by 1950.*

Left and Below: *Practical experience showed that plunging shells could penetrate the often weakly armored decks of warships (as happened to HMS* Hood*) and to achieve this howitzers, with their higher trajectories were perfect. To this end a developmental 16-inch M1918 howitzer was built (***Below left***) with a 15-cal barrel. It proved too short for accurate use so another massive piece of coastal artillery, the 16-inch howitzer M1920 (406 mm) was designed in 1918. With a 25-cal barrel and a special barbette mounting similar to that used on the 16-inch/50 M1919 gun. Four were built because the war ended. All of them went to Fort Story, VA as part of the Chesapeake Bay defenses. As with so many other of the big gun defenses, they didn't fire a shot in anger and were scrapped in 1947.*

Chapter 4: World War II

Opposite: *Battery Way was a battery of four 12-inch mortars located on the island of Corregidor. Battery Way was one of two (Battery Geary the other) mortar batteries at Fort Mills that, with Fort Hughes, Fort Drum, Fort Frank, and Fort Wint formed the Harbor Defenses of Manila and Subic Bays. Battery Way was named for Lt. Henry N. Way of the 4th US Artillery.*

Only twenty years separate the two largest wars the world has ever witnessed (so far). Obviously the root causes that brought about the first furious onslaught had not changed much since 1914–1918, because in 1939–1945 almost exactly the same thing happened all over again—this time on an even larger scale with increasingly sophisticated armament industries producing ever more lethal weapons culminating in the very industrialization of death and destruction. So many new weapons systems were being invented that it would take some time and a lot of combat before all the implications worked themselves out. Certainly the search for superweapons continued—the elusive knockout blow that all combatants dream of and struggle for—but what form would it take? The major industrialized states continued their weapons research programs (especially a resentful Germany, who wasn't supposed to), with their different geographical locations dictating their preoccupations with certain specific types of ordnance. Nations with long coastlines concentrated more on their navies and coastal fortifications, while continental countries were primarily concerned with fortified lines of defense, fortresses, and ever larger artillery to smash them.

Since the last cataclysm mechanized warfare had come into its own with self-propelled gasoline-fueled vehicles on tracks and wheels—armored cars, guns, troops carriers, and of course, tanks, whose use was now a radical game changer, all brought highly mobile intensity to the battlefield. However it must be remembered that these changes weren't simultaneous or universal—some armies were still dependent on horses as well—especially to haul artillery. It is often forgotten that for the German invasion of Russia ('Barbarossa') as many horses were deployed as motor vehicles.

Air power that had been a fledgling in the last war became a major arm in its own right and like armor went on to transform the battlefield. Waiting not too far in the future was missile technology that would eventually take over the role of superlarge long-range weapons, but for now artillery was a vital component in all its forms and big guns were still prized. Ammunition had also advanced dramatically since World War I with a selection of rounds for different targets—shaped charges like HEAT (high explosive anti-tank) and HESH (high explosive squash head), tungsten-cored armor-piercing, fragmentation, white phosphorous and delayed fused anti-aircraft. 128mm anti-aircraft guns could reach aircraft as high as 30,000ft using a new type of slow-burning propellant invented by the Germans. The proximity fuse (that automatically detonates when the distance to a target becomes smaller than a preset figure) was a joint British and American development for air defense and later for air burst against ground targets.

With all these different assets to consider and choose from, what was invested in depended on the mindset and resources of each nation, decided while closely monitoring their opponents' efforts. The war fought on the world stage and almost every continent required different weapons for different theaters and lots of them, so in the end it became a war of supply and production—the logistics, the resources

SIGNAL CORPS
U.S. ARMY

SIGNAL CORPS

and how wisely they were spent. Perhaps it is easy with the benefit of hindsight to see where mistakes were made.

All the major powers continued to maintain some super-heavy artillery—usually in the form of railroad guns—in the interwar period, despite the growing threat of bomber aircraft. The United States mainly used them as a supplement to fixed coastal defense artillery. Britain only had a handful to provide additional back up defenses along the Channel coast where invasion threatened. Russia used a few railroad guns against the Finns and, later, the Germans, but concentrated on producing a huge quantity of smaller caliber heavy field artillery pieces. France had old railroad guns left over from the last war and had mounted massive ex-naval guns in various forts but had a shortage of modern mobile heavy artillery, the largest French gun being the 155mm (6-inch) GPF rifle.

Where would superguns be without the Germans? Despite the destruction of much of their World War I matériel and crippling reparations, they were still intent on developing the biggest guns they could. Once the superweapon-loving Nazi regime came to power in 1933, weapons' production went into overdrive and Germany made a bewildering number of different railroad superguns in a relatively short space of time. The quickest to appear were, again, surplus naval guns between 150 and 280mm (5.9 and 11-inch) from World War I battleships that could be adapted quickly such as the 240mm (9.5-inch) SK L/30 "Theodor Otto" and the 240mm "Theodor" Kanone (E). Some of these guns still relied solely on track curvature to aim properly, but others were fitted with a Vögele turntable (invented towards the end of World War I) enabling the gun to pivot on a central mount and have full traverse—though with circular rails required to rotate the outer edges. Of all the railroad guns ever manufactured the 280mm (11-inch) Kanone 5 (E) was, perhaps, the most successful. It first entered service in 1936 and remained in production throughout the war until 1945, seeing action on all fronts. Other large German guns developed were mounted in the howitzer and mortar styles designed for high-elevation, siege, long-range bombardment and ,counter-battery fire. The 170mm (6.7-inch) K18 Mörser proved to be one of the best guns of the war, while the 210mm (8.3-inch) Lange Mörser 18 and the 210mm (8.3-inch) Mörser 18 (Brümmbar) were never manufactured in any great numbers. Germany went on to produce the largest land gun ever built and used in combat—the 800mm (31.5-inch) *Kanone Eisenbahnlafette Gustav Gerät* or 80cm K (E). This monster weapon weighed 1,350 tons and fired a seven-ton concrete-piercing shell to a range of 23 miles. It was used successfully on the Eastern Front against Sebastapol and with it a high watermark for this kind of weapon was reached. The Germans also scavenged and reused many weapons that they captured from their enemies, especially French and Soviet artillery, even manufacturing the ammunition to fit.

Many of the largest weapons (battleship main guns) went into the emplacements of the Atlantic Wall, which represented a colossal effort of time and resources while yielding questionable results. When it came to the reckoning, these behemoths in concrete caissons took up far too many raw materials and too much work and most barely saw any action, though the guns closest to the British coast in the Pas de Calais managed

Opposite: *Italian proving ground overrun by US troops during World War II.*

Below: *Railway gun projectiles.*

to inflict some damage and disruption to shipping. The German coastal guns around the Normandy area of Fortress Europe were engaged by various Allied weapons—by air, sea and land. Most lasted less than twenty-four hours. Defending a border from the Arctic Circle to Spain was impossible and took up so many resources. Take the Channel Islands: the massive array of artillery, the huge control and observation towers, the large garrison—all of it sidelined military resources that just weren't used.

As the war progressed lack of raw materials became a critical issue for Germany. Once the tide turned there was a gradual attrition of quantity and quality, both in the guns which were kept in desperate overuse and in the crews whose hard-learned expertise was lost when they were thrown away as ground troops in extremis. The strategic bombing campaign sapped their industrial strength and terrorized their population. The Germans had no strategic bombers: their projection of military power when it arrived came in the form of rockets.

Below: *USS* North Carolina *(BB55) was typical of the new breed of fast battleships laid down in the late 1930s but still subject to the treaty limitations of 35,000 tons displacement and guns no larger than 16in caliber.*

On the immediate battlefield the *Nebelwerfer* and *Katushya* rocket launchers had brought the modern return of an ancient weapon: one now more accurate and more deadly. Any loss of precision was more than catered for by their use en masse, where the incredible noise itself became a psychologically devastating weapon that intimidated the enemy, besides being able to saturate a huge area in high explosive. (They are still in use today as the MLRS multi-launch rocket system.) But it was the V-weapons appearing towards the end of World War II heralded a new age of missile technology. There was no getting away from the fact that local heavy artillery was still essential to support troops both in attack and defense, but longer-range targets now didn't require a supergun or a bomber force if a missile could do the job. The problem for Germany was that the superweapons appeared too late and they had neither the wherewithal to build them—being forced to use slave labor under the Harz mountains—nor safe places to launch them. Allied air superiority ensured that V-1 and V-2 sites were bombarded wherever they were seen

Naval Weapons

In the aftermath of World War I the major naval powers all planned a new generation of larger and more powerfully armed capital ships. These included the British 48,500-ton "G3" class battlecruisers, the American 43,200-ton "South Dakota" class battleships and the Japanese 41,200-ton "Amagi" class battlecruisers, all to be armed with 16-inch guns. In addition other projected designs by all three nations included 18-inch or even 20-inch guns. The cost of such ships in peacetime was not a realistic proposition, and in an effort to prevent the sort of naval arms race which was an important factor in the lead up to World War I, a conference of the naval powers was held in 1921 and resulted in the 1922 Washington Naval Treaty. It set overall tonnage limits which resulted in a substantial reduction in the size of the British and American battle fleets and also restricted the size of any future capital ships to 35,000 tons (standard displacement) as well as limiting the caliber of main armament to 16-inch guns. Finally, and subject to some specific exceptions, no signatory nation was permitted to lay down or complete any new battleships or battlecruisers during a ten-year building "holiday." The 1936 London Naval Treaty subsequently lowered main armament to 14-inch guns and the British "King George V" class laid down in 1937 were so armed. However, as Japan did not ratify this treaty its provisions were not binding, and the US Navy adopted 16-inch guns for the "North Carolina" class also laid down in 1937. In doing so it assumed that new Japanese battleships then planned would be armed with 16-inch guns, and it was not until 1945 that it was discovered that the two "Yamato" class laid down in great secrecy in 1937–1938 were, in fact ,mounting 18-inch guns.

Other new battleships laid down in the 1930s by France Italy, and Germany were mostly armed with 15-inch guns, although France also completed the two "Dunkerque" class armed with 13.4-inch guns and the projected German "H" class battleships (1938) would have carried 16-inch guns. The projected British "Lion" class would also have mounted 16-inch guns but these were canceled in 1939.

The advent of aircraft carriers changed the face of naval warfare in the course of World War II. In 1939 the battleship was still regarded in many quarters as the ultimate arbiter of sea power and the aircraft carrier was untested in action. However, by 1945 naval air power reigned supreme and the role of the battleship was relegated to secondary duties such as protecting the carriers and supporting amphibious operations. Consequently, surface actions between capital ships were relatively uncommon, the best known being the engagements between the *Bismarck* and elements of the British Home Fleet in May 1941. Although *Bismarck*'s 15-inch guns destroyed the battlecruiser *Hood*, she was herself completely wrecked by the 14-inch and 16-inch guns of HMS *King George V* and HMS *Rodney*. Then, in December 1943, HMS *Duke of York* sank the German battlecruiser *Scharnhorst*. In November 1942 the Japanese battleship *Hiei* was disabled by the 16-inch guns of USS *Washington* and was subsequently finished off by air attacks. The last engagement between battleships was in October 1944 when, in the Leyte Gulf battles, the Japanese battleship *Yamashiro* was sunk in the Surigao Straits by the gunfire of six battleships of the US 7th Fleet (all survivors of Pearl Harbor). The USS *Mississippi*, armed with twelve 14-inch guns, is credited with the last salvo ever fired from one battleship against another. It was the end of an era in naval warfare.

Below: *A sketch showing the appearance of the 43,200-ton "South Dakota" class battleships which were laid down in 1920–1921. Armed with no less than twelve 16in guns all six were canceled and scrapped before launching under the terms of the Washington Treaty.*

Forts and Castles: The Twentieth Century

*Examples of the Maginot Line. Schoenenbourg (***Below***) Based on the* fort palmé *approach with no clearly defined perimeter, interlocking fields of fire from casemates and turrets connected by underground passages (exemplified by Michelsberg* **Below Right***) excavated at an average depth of around 100ft. They join to a common barracks and entrance in the rear. Close defense was provided by ditches, barbed wire, machine guns, flamethrowers and, above all, the fire of other fortifications.*

Even the most prescient military writer would have struggled to contemplate how everything would change during the twentieth century. The Crimean, American Civil, and Franco-Prussian wars had pointers—sieges, railways, trenches, forts, balloons, the Gatling gun, mines, big gun bombardments—but little could have prepared the world for aerial and airborne warfare, submarine warfare, machine guns, the eclipse of cavalry and their replacement by tanks and vehicles, guided missiles and drones, and atomic weapons.

The static warfare of World War I was the crucible of much of this change. A global conflict, it saw the development of weapons that rendered traditional strongpoints useless. Out went anything that could be bombarded by artillery or bombed from the air. In came trench warfare, machine guns, barbed wire, and deep shelters. But between the wars the past reasserted itself: the creation of the Maginot line and the Atlantic Wall, and all other such defenses, proved ineffective in World War II. Reinforced concrete, steel cupolas, underground networks: none of these were able to withstand the new ways of waging war. Eben Emael, Normandy's beach defenses, the Westwall: none of these worked.

And then, two events rendered all military defenses to date superfluous: the launch of the first V–2 in 1944 brought the delivery system; the cataclysm of the atomic bomb brought the destructive power. What chance fixed defense against such power? The only way to stop ICBMs is through technology: early warning systems, anti-missile defenses, Star Wars. Today's castles are for police actions and asymmetric warfare.

Left: *Casemate Vincent de Groot at Fort Eben-Emael. The fort fell to an airborne coup de main as gliders, led by Rudolf Witzig, silently landed on the roof of the fortress and took the defenders by surprise. They used hollow charges to destroy or disable the gun cupolas and a flamethrower against the machine guns.*

Below: *Machine-gun cupolas at Verdun's Fort Douaumont.*

Below: *Hanička is a Czech artillery fort, and part of the defensive system completed in 1938. It was surrendered without a fight to Wehrmacht soldiers, which then tested the strength of the Czech guns. Postwar the underground facilities were adapted and equipped as a government survival shelter.*

Right: *The Atlantic Wall saw a huge amount of German resources wasted on complex concrete structures that today pay mute testimony to the period. This is WN 126 Batterie Blankense at Néville-sur-Mer east of Cherbourg. It had casemates for four 9.4cm M39(e) guns and a variety of bunkers.*

1927: Royal Navy BL 16-inch/45-cal Mk. I Guns

The largest naval guns available to the Royal Navy during World War II were the 16-inch guns mounted in the battleships HMS *Nelson* and HMS *Rodney*. These had been laid down in 1923 in the aftermath of the Washington Treaty and consequently were limited to a maximum 35,000 tons displacement. Effectively they were cut down versions of the 48,000-ton battlecruisers projected at the end of World War I. Each was armed with nine 16-inch/45-cal Mk. I guns in three triple turrets which were all grouped forward of the bridge so that the maximum armor protection could be applied to the combined magazines within the displacement available. Each gun weighed 108 tons and fired a 2,048lb shell to a maximum range of 39,884yd using cordite propellant made of up to six 100lb charges each contained in silk bags. The total rotating mass of the Mk. I triple mounting, including the three guns, was 1,420 tons and with the availability of new more precise fire control systems the guns could be elevated to forty degrees in order to achieve the maximum range potential. However this feature necessitated a very complex loading cycle for which the guns had to be lowered to the three-degree position between each firing. Initially the loading mechanisms suffered teething problems but most of these had been remedied by May 27, 1941, when *Rodney*'s guns caused severe and significant damage to the German battleship *Bismarck*, which was left in floundering before being finished off with torpedoes.

Below: *HMS* Nelson *was one of two 35,000-ton/ 16-inch gun battleships which Britain was permitted to build under the terms of the Washington Treaty. Both were laid down in December 1922 and the grouping of the main armament forward in three triple turrets was adopted to keep overall displacement within treaty limits.*

16-INCH MK. 1 GUN

20th Century
Great Britain
Makers: Armstrong Whitworth; Vickers; William Beardmore & Co; Royal Gun Factory

Barrel length: 60ft
Weight: 108 tons
Caliber: 16 inches (406mm)
Max range: 22.6 miles

Above and Right: *HMS* Rodney*'s battery of nine 16-inch/45-cal guns makes an imposing sight in this posed prewar view. In 1941 these guns were used with terrible effect against the German battleship* Bismarck.

1930: Japanese Type 90 240mm Railroad Gun

TYPE 90 240MM RAILROAD GUN

20th Century
Japan/France
Maker: Schneider and Saint-Chamond (of cannon)/other equipment Japanese
Location: none extant

Barrel length: 42 feet
Weight: 136 tons
Caliber: 240mm (9.45 inches)
Max range: 31 miles

The Type 90 240mm gun was a Japanese heavy weapon, and the only one they possessed. The gun was bought from France in 1930 and then mounted onto a Japanese-designed carriage and auxiliary equipment.

France's TLP (*très longue portée*—Very Long Range) project had been rationalized after the Armistice and involved experimenting with canceled battleship barrels. Two of the largest French arms manufacturers, Schneider and Saint-Chamond, made various prototypes to test. Schneider experienced problems with their gun barrel wear, breech overpressure, low velocity, and poor range, Relining and smoothbore barrel extensions solved some of these problems but by the time World War II no definitive weapon had been produced. Schneider also reused existing railway carriages to mount their guns so their traverse was dependent on rail curvature.

Saint-Chamond took a different approach and designed a new carriage with a central turntable and full traverse using a 240mm L/51 gun achieving a range up to 64,500yd. In 1924 the two companies merged and this prototype was then sold to Japan in 1930. The Japanese first used it as an addition to the coastal defense of Tokyo Bay but in 1941 it was deployed to Manchuria where it saw brief action before being destroyed by the Japanese army as they retreated at the end of the war. The Type 90 fired HE shells up to a range of 31 miles.

Right: *A Schneider 240mm-caliber railroad gun in France. An example of this gun was sold to Japan where it was designated the Type 90.*

Above Left: *The Japanese had a number other large weapons. This 280mm coast defense howitzer had a maximum range of approximately 8,300yd.*

Above: *The Type 45 (1912) 240mm howitzer had a range of 11,000yd.*

Left: *The Type 90 railroad gun.*

1938: Krupp 210mm K12 (E) Railroad Gun

210MM K12 (E)

20th Century
Germany
Maker: Krupp
Location: none extant

Length: 109ft 3in
Weight: 297.28 tons
Caliber: 210mm (8.31in)
Max range: 71.5 miles

Below: *Krupp K12 (E) about to fire.*

The *21cm Kanone 12 in Eisenbahnlafette* (*21cm K 12 (E)*) was mounted on a simple box-girder carriage, which was carried on two subframes in turn mounted on double bogies. The barrel was mounted in a ring cradle with a hydropneumatic recoil system. The barrel's extreme length required external bracing to prevent it from bending under its own weight. Its trunnions were placed as far forward as possible to balance the barrel and minimize the force necessary to elevate it. This placed the breech perilously close to the ground and a hydraulic jacking system was built in each subframe to elevate the mount by a meter (3.3ft). However it was impossible to load the weapon in this position and it had to be lowered between every shot. The K 12 (E) could be fired from any curved section of track, a Vögele turntable, or from its special firing track. This prefabricated T-shaped track was carried on the gun train and deployed by a special crane wagon.

The first weapon was completed in 1938 and delivered to the Heer in March 1939. It was successful, although the necessity to jack it up and down between shots was not well received by the army. Krupp discovered, on trying to rectify this problem, that hydropneumatic balancing-presses could work at much greater weights and pressures than previously believed. They redesigned the mounting with the trunnions as far forward as possible and increased the recoil stroke to 59 inches. The new design was delivered during the summer of 1940 and called the K 12 N (E). The first gun was retrospectively called the K 12 V (E).

They spent the war assigned to Artillerie-Batterie 701 (E) along the Channel coast. The British recovered shell fragments near Chatham, Kent, some 55 miles from the nearest point on the French coast.

1938: Krupp 280mm K5 (E) Railroad Gun

KRUPP K5 (E)

20th Century
Germany
Maker: Krupp
Location: Batterie Todt Museum, France; US Army Ordnance Museum, Fort Lee, USA

Length: 70ft 1in
Weight: 214.59 tons
Caliber: 280mm (11.14 inches)
Max range: 40 miles

Development began in the mid-1930s of the Krupp 280mm (11-inch) Kanone 5 (E), also known as the K5 *Tiefzug*. This became perhaps the most successful German railroad gun of World War II, being made and used throughout its duration and seeing action on almost all fronts. The K5 was first used in the 1940 invasion of France where there were problems with splitting barrels which were solved by changes to the rifling of the bore. Late in the war a couple of K5s were modified with smoothbore 310mm (12.2- inch) barrels in order to fire a rocket-assisted projectiles known as *Peenemünder Pfeilgeschosse* flechettes.

The K5 had a caliber of 283mm (11.1-inch) firing two types of shell, the G35 weighing 562lb or the G39 weighing 584lb at a rate of about fifteen shots an hour. Traverse was achieved through track curvature or more precisely through the addition of the 360-degree Vögele turntable with the gun jacked up on platform rotated with the aid of circular rails.

Two K5s saw successful action in Italy in 1944 against the American landings at Anzio. Known as "Leopold" and "Robert" by their crews and "Anzio Annie" and "Anzio Express" by Allied soldiers, they bombarded the small beachhead for almost four months inflicting massive damage.

When not in use they were hidden in tunnels. The two guns were finally incapacitated by the Germans themselves when they retreated and were captured on June 7, 1944. "Leopold" was taken back to America and can be seen at the United States Army Ordnance Museum in Fort Lee, Petersburg, Virginia. Another K5 (E) is at the Batterie Todt Museum at Audinghen, France. (See photo below.)

Below Left: *Turm I of the four huge Battery Todt casemates, which housed 380mm guns, provides the setting for the Atlantic Wall Museum and outside is a German Krupp K5 railroad gun.*

Below: *K5 in 1941 on the Atlantic Wall moving out of its shelter in Hydrequent, northern France.*

This Page: *The K5 gun displayed at the Battery Todt, Audinghen.*

Other German Railroad Guns

During World War II, Germany was the premier builder and user of superheavy railroad guns. By 1945 Allied intelligence identified some twelve different types of German-made railroad artillery, ranging from 150mm to 800mm. Captured Czech and French pieces were also widely used. Over forty guns were produced by Germany during the war, and captured weapons (especially the French ones) were co-opted into service.

German railway artillery over 200mm included: the 240mm guns "Theodor" and "Theodor Bruno"; the 274mm K(E) 592(f) L/46.7 (the French Schneider); at 280mm "kurze Bruno," "lange Bruno," "schwere Bruno," "Bruno neue," and K5(E); two French 340mm guns designated 673(f) and 370mm howitzer 711(f); the 380mm "Siegfried" and 406mm "Adolf"; and the French 520mm howitzer 871(f).

In spite of the Red Army's advance into Poland, the Germans continued to deploy railroad guns and Karl-series caterpillar-tracked mortars to pummel Warsaw during the uprising of late summer 1944. Many were captured during the advances through France and Italy, by which time the Reich had turned to the V-weapons as their long-range weapon of choice.

Below Left: *A 274mm K(E) 592(f)—a French Schneider 274mm (1917)—was lost in the Montelimar Pocket as Allied forces advanced north from the Operation Dragoon landings in the south of France.*

Above: *Men of 11th Armored Division inspect a 240mm gun captured at Kulmbach, Germany in 1945.*

Below: *There were four 203mm K(E) railway guns at Auderville-Laye to the west of Cherbourg using Vögele turntables.*

Left: *"Anzio Annie" at Aberdeen Proving Grounds.*

Below Left: *240mm K(E) "Theodor Bruno" captured at Torigni-sur-Vire, August 1944.*

Below: *240mm rail gun knocked out in 1944.*

1939: USSR 280mm Mortar M1939 (Br-5)

As with all massive howitzers the M1939 (Br-5) has something of the ancient bombard about it. It was introduced in 1939 and continued in service with the Red Army into the 1970s. Despite its tracked self-propulsion, the heaviest artillery gun in the Soviet arsenal was a cumbersome weapon whose great weight made it very difficult to move off-road and as a result it saw action only occasionally. However, when used in the classic fort-killing mode—as in the Red Army's final assault on Nazi Berlin in 1945—the M1939 was very effective, its massive shells obliterating any obstacles.

It fired HE and AP shells weighing 370lb and had a crew of fifteen men. It had a relatively slow rate of fire because the barrel required regular cooling—but it laeft a crater thirty-foot deep.

Other Soviet superheavy weapons of World War II included the 210mm (8.3-inch) Gun M1939 (Br-17) and the 305mm (12-inch) Howitzer M1939 (Br-18)—both Czech heavy artillery made by Skoda, the designs of which had been sold to the Soviets by the Germans under the Molotov-Ribbentrop Pact when they occupied Czechoslovakia in 1939. Very few were built, but those that were saw action in the defense of Leningrad 1941–1944. Both guns used the same carriage, firing platform and control mechanisms. The 210mm Br-17 weighed 95,279lb, had a barrel length of 30ft, and fired shells weighing 297lb to a range of 18.24 miles. The 305mm Br-18 weighed 101,000lb, had a barrel length of 22 feet), and fired shells to a range of 18,133yd.

280MM M1939 (BR-5)

20th Century
Soviet Union
Maker: Barrikady
Location: St Petersburg Artillery Museum, Russia

Barrel length: 16ft
Weight: 40,565lb
Caliber: 8.3 inches
Max range: 6.8 miles

Right: *Soviet 280mm Br-5 Mark 1939 mortar, displayed in Saint Petersburg Artillery Museum. Photo taken on March 3, 2007.*

1939: Rheinmetall 355mm M1 Howitzer

355MM M1 HOWITZER

20th Century
Germany
Maker: Rheinmetall
Location: none extant

Barrel length: 31ft 5in
Weight: 73.83 tons
Caliber: 355mm (14.02 inches)
Max range: 13 miles
Max range: 13,000 yards

Designed in 1936 by Rheinmetall-Borsig and first produced in 1939, the 355mm (14-inch) *Haubitze* M1 was a heavy siege howitzer made by Rheinmetall up to 1944. It was a sunsible enlargement of the 240mm K3. Though only eight were built in total, they had a busy war being used in the 1940 assault on Belgian and French fortresses, then on the Eastern front in Operation Barbarossa, at the sieges of Sebastopol and Leningrad, and later to bombard the city during the Warsaw Uprising. The gun traveled unassembled in half a dozen trailers usually towed by SdKfz 9 halftracks and including a generator-powered gantry cane required for reassembly, which took about two hours. The generator could also be used as an ammunition hoist and to elevate the weapon.

The *Haubitze* M1 had a hydropneumatic dual recoil system where both the gun and its mount moved separately to absorb the gun's blast. It also had a two part carriage system for easier portability that could be jacked up and fitted to a turntable for all-round traverse. It fired HE shells weighing 1,270lb, and an AP concrete-busting shell with a ballistic cap weighing 2,042lb to a range of 22,800yd. The elevation span was +45 to +75 degrees. During peak usage, an M1 crew had a rate-of-fire of one round in four to five minutes.

Right: *The 355mm* Haubitze *(Howitzer) M1 saw service in the battle of France and spent the rest of the war on the Eastern Front, participating in Operation Barbarossa, the sieges of Sebastopol and Leningrad, and helped to put down the Warsaw Uprising in 1944.*

1940: Rheinmetall 600mm/540mm Karl-Gerät Mortar 040/041

With the Maginot Line and other heavy European fortifications in mind Germany continued to research and build superlarge weapons. In 1936 Rheinmetall began work on what would become the giant self-propelled Karl-Gerät Mortar. Altogether six guns were produced in two versions between 1940–1941 (040 and 041) and saw combat in the German invasion of Russia, Warsaw and elsewhere in Europe during the German retreat. As was usual with all really big guns each was given a name—*Adam*, *Eva*, *Thor*, *Odin*, *Loki*, and *Ziu*. Each "Karl" weighed 139 tons and required its own set of heavy transport trailers, an ammunition-loading crane, and several ammunition carriers. The original 040 version had a short barrel with a caliber of 600mm (24-inch), fired concrete-piercing shells to a range of 4,720yd. The 041 version had a longer gun with a lighter caliber of 540mm (21-inch) to increase its range to 11,000yd. Both versions had to be loaded at zero elevation and so reaimed each time before firing.

The Karl-Geräts were self-propelled on tracks using a twelve-cylinder Daimler-Benz MB503A gasoline or a MB 507C diesel engine after 1944, however, with a speed of 6.3mph this was mainly used for positional fine tuning and traverse. To travel long distances the gun was disassembled and transported by rail on several trucks. Before firing it required carefully selected solid ground that had been prepared and leveled.

From the combat histories of the Karl-Geräts their use was only intermittently successful. They saw action mainly on the Eastern Front, used in siege operation like Sebastopol and Leningrad, but there were problems with barrel explosions, supply and maintenance of essential parts, continual relocation and transport. They were a time-consuming precious resource to be guarded at all costs to prevent them falling into enemy hands. Nonetheless they did. In 1945, *Eva* and *Loki* were captured by US forces along with the original unnamed test weapon while *Ziu* and *Odin* were captured by the Russian Army. The fate of *Adam* and *Thor* remains unknown.

600MM KARL-GERÄT MORTAR 040/041

20th Century
Germany
Maker: Rheinmetall
Location: Kubinka Tank Museum, Moscow, Russia

Barrel length: 040–13ft 9in; 041–20ft 2.5in
Weight: 124 tons
Caliber: 040–600mm (24 inches); 041–254mm (21 inches)
Max range: 040–2.6 miles); 041–6.2 miles

Above Left: *The Karl-Gerät needed its own ammunition carrier (on a PzKpfw IV chassis), seen here next to* Odin. *Each shell was twenty-four inches in diameter and weighed 4,800lb.*

Below Left: Ziu *was captured by the Red Army, probably when they overran Jüterbog on April 20, 1945. Held at the Russian tank museum, when they prepared the vehicle for repainting the name* Adam *was found underneath and that's how it is displayed.*

1940: Royal Navy BL 14-inch Mk. VII Gun

Apart from specified exceptions, the terms of the 1922 Washington Treaty placed an embargo on the construction of new battleships for a period of ten years and the subsequent London Naval Conference proposed the mounting of guns no larger than 14-inch caliber. By early 1937, with war clouds gathering, the Royal Navy was desperate to lay down the first of five "King George V" class battleships but with the treaty limitations still in force, these ships were designed to be armed with a new 14-inch gun. To compensate for the reduced caliber (compared to the previous 15-inch gun) the new ships were to be armed with twelve 14-inch guns in three quadruple turrets. In the event it was necessary to reduce this to ten guns in two quadruple and one twin mounting in order to remain within the 35,000-ton displacement treaty limitation. In an attempt to allay public concern about the reduced caliber it was officially stated that the new guns had a greater range (36,322yd) than the older 15-inch guns. While this was factually correct, it was only due to the fact that the new mounting permitted a forty-degree elevation compared to twenty degrees in the older ships. Each individual Mk. VII gun weighed 79 tons ,while the total rotating mass of the Mk. III quadruple mounting was 1,500 tons and that of the Mk. II twin was 900 tons. Weight of the projectile was 1,590lb—considerably less than the 1,920lb of contemporary British 15-inch shells. By the time the first two ships (*King George V* and *Prince of Wales*) were commissioned in 1940–1941, they were urgently needed so there was no time to remedy the inevitable defects of the new mountings.

Consequently, in the *Bismarck* engagement *Prince of Wales* was forced to break off the action due to a defective turret after the battlecruiser *Hood* had been sunk while *King George V* was eventually reduced to only two serviceable guns by the end of the final action. However these difficulties were slowly overcome and HMS *Duke of York* fared better on December 26, 1943, when her guns were responsible for sinking the German battlecruiser *Scharnhorst*.

BL 14-inch Mk. VII Gun

20th Century
Great Britain
Maker: Elswick Ordnance Company

Barrel length: 53ft 7in
Weight: 79 tons
Caliber: 14 inches (356mm)
Max range: 20.6 miles

Opposite: *HMS* Anson *shows her full battery of ten 14-inch guns trained to starboard in preparation for a postwar training shoot.*

Left: *The forward 14-inch turrets of the British battleship HMS* King George V. *Strict observance of the Washington Treaty displacement limits resulted in the unusual arrangement of one quadruple and one twin mounting instead of the originally intended two quadruple turrets.*

1940: Krupp 406mm SK C/34 and 380mm SK C/34 Guns

The 42,200-ton battleships *Bismarck* and *Tirpitz* (completed in 1940 and 1941) were each armed with eight 380mm/50-cal SK C/34 guns. These each weighed 109 tons and fired a 1,764lb AP shell to a range of 39,800yd at thirty degress of elevation and rate of fire was slightly better than two rounds per minute. The revolving mass of the twin turret was 1,047 tons. The effectiveness of these guns was dramatically demonstrated in May 1941 when a shell from *Bismarck*'s fifth salvo fired at a range of approximately 14,000yd penetrated *Hood*'s armor and set off a magazine explosion which sank the ship.

Although there were only the two 15-inch armed battleships, the German Navy also had the three "Deutschland" class armored ships (popularly known as pocket battleships) and the two "Scharnhorst" class battlecruisers. These were all armed with versions of the 280mm (11-inch) gun, a caliber which had armed many of German World War I battlecruisers. Although not a heavyweight when compared to contemporary 15-inch and 16-inch guns, it was a remarkably effective weapon. The SK

Left: *The forward triple turret of the German* Panzerschiffe Deutschland *(later renamed* Lützow*) which housed three 280mm/52-cal SK C/28 guns. The later battlecruisers* Scharnhorst *and* Gneisenau *were armed with the slightly improved SK C/34 280mm (11.1-inch) gun in three triple mountings.*

C/34 variant mounted by *Scharnhorst* and *Gneisenau* fired a 727lb shell to a range of over 44,760yd at a thirty-degree elevation, substantially greater than the 36,500yd achievable by the 14-inch guns in the British *King George V* class. Indeed, postwar research credits *Scharnhorst* with hitting the aircraft carrier HMS *Glorious* in 1940 off Norway at a range in excess of 26,000yd, equaling HMS *Warspite*'s claim to longest ranged hit in naval warfare.

Although never built, Germany did plan to arm the projected "H" class battleships with 406mm (16-inch) SK C/34 guns (sometimes known as the *Adolfkanone* (Adolf gun) and even envisaged 100,000-ton battleships armed with 508mm (20-inch) guns. One example of an even larger 530mm (21-inch) gun was test-fired and was expected to fire a 4,850lb shell to a range of over 50,000yd although any intended naval application was unclear.

380MM SK C/34 GUN

20th Century
Germany
Maker: Krupp
Location: Fort Møvik, Norway (in turret); Hanstholm, Denmark (barrel only)

Length: 64ft 5in
Weight: 109 tons
Caliber: 380mm (15 inches)
Max range: 34.6 miles

Below: *Pride of the Kriegsmarine in 1941 was the newly commissioned 42,000-ton battleship* Bismarck *armed with eight 380mm (15-inch) guns. Although successfully sinking the battlecruiser HMS* Hood *with only six salvoes on May 24, 1941, she was sunk only three days later by the combined fire of HMS* King George V *and HMS* Rodney. *A modified version of these guns was used by various coastal artillery batteries including one at Cap Gris Nez.*

Left and Below: *Today's Fort Møvik in Norway was called* Batterie Vara *by the Germans. It was heavily armed with four 380mm SK C/34 guns with a range of twenty-six miles, one in a turret (***Below***) and the others on S169 emplacements (***Left***) which were dismantled during the 1960s. The guns were tasked with guarding the Skagerrak in conjunction with their sister battery at Hanstholm (see next page) in Denmark, some seventy miles across the strait. Another SK C/34 turret—a triple, the B turret of the* Gneisenau *as part of MKB 11./504 Fjell on Sotra island—defended the approaches to Bergen.*

Right: *As elsewhere, surplus naval guns often found themselves used as railway guns. Here a 380mm "Siegfried" gun of Eisenbahn-Batterie 698, this one named* Gneisenau, *whose gun would have been used on a "Bismarck" class pocket battleship.*

Below Right: *The Lindemann Battery on Cap Gris Nez, France, named in honor of the captain of the battleship* Bismarck, *had three 406mm SK C/34 guns in 50ft high concrete emplacements. They fired over 2,000 shells across the Channel at Dover. Heavily bombed, the Lindemann Battery sustained little damage until one turret was hit on September 3, 1944, by a shell from a British railway gun.*

Below: *Hanstholm II battery in Denmark, across the Skagerrak from Kristiansund (see p.180), had four SK C/34 guns intended for the* Gneisenau *giving the battery the firepower to protect the southern side of the straits. The guns were scrapped in the early 1950s, but the emplacements are still there today, part of an impressive museum. Outside the museum are three weapons: a barrel for one of the 380mm guns (nearest the camera), a 150mm turret and in the distance, a Russian 122mm.*

Right and Opposite: Gneisenau*'s "C"—Caesar—turret at Fort Austrått. Today the rangefinder for the battery is near the* Gneisenau *turret.*

Below Right: *MKB 5/511 Trondenes in Norway was armed with four* 406mm *SK C/34 guns made for the "H" class battleships that weren't built. Three of the guns were ready for action in May 1943; the last in August. As elsewhere in Norway, the heavy labor at Trondenes was carried out by Russian PoWs, who were treated extremely poorly.*

406MM SK C/34 VARIANT

20th Century
Germany
Maker: Krupp
Location: Three-gun turret in Trondenes, Norway

Barrel length: 60ft 4.6in
Weight: 122 tons
Caliber: 406mm (16 inches)
Max range: 25.4 miles

1941: Krupp 800mm *Schwerer Gustav* Railroad Gun

800MM SCHWERER GUSTAV RAILROAD GUN

20th Century
Germany
Maker: Krupp
Location: Railway Museum, Utrecht (model)

Barrel length: 106ft 7in
Weight: 1,328,90 tons
Caliber: 800mm
(31.5 inches)
Max range: 28.9 miles (HE); 23.8 miles (AP)

Schwerer Gustav has the distinction of being the biggest and heaviest gun ever built and used in the world to date. Although both the British Mallett's Mortar and the American Little David Mortar had a larger, 36-inch caliber neither gun ever saw action or got beyond a test-firing stage. *Schwerer Gustav* was the biggest mobile artillery with the largest caliber ever used in combat and fired the heaviest shells ever made. A classic castle killer, expressly designed in the mid-1930s for the destruction of the powerful French defenses of the Maginot Line, construction problems with the gigantic barrel meant that it missed the 1940 battle of France. Completed in 1941 it ultimately saw action on Eastern Front where its performance was brief but spectacular.

This behemoth weighed 1,490 tons had a total length of 155ft and a L/40.6 barrel length of 106.8ft. It fired two types of shell, HE weighing 10,600lb to a range of 51,000yd and AP weighing 15,700lb to a range of 42,000yd. After approximately 300 shells the barrel needed relining so there were at least two spares while the old one was sent back to Germany for renewal. It required a crew of about 450 to assemble and operate the weapon, although if you include the workforce needed to build extra rail spurs and firing positions and the anti-aircraft and guard units, this brought the total up to 5,000 men. To traverse it required the usual dual circular track to be doubled. The gun's massive bulk meant it traveled unassembled in five carriages of a train of twenty-five coaches complete with crew, cranes, and ammunition. Steven Zaloga quotes the building cost of each vehicle as being the same as twenty-five Tiger tanks.

Its moment of glory came in 1942 at the siege of Sebastopol in the Crimea where, using a reconnaissance aircraft to direct fire, its colossal shells destroyed coastal guns, several forts, an undersea ammunition depot, and along with other heavy artillery reduced the city to ruins. It was moved at different times to be used against both Leningrad and Stalingrad but was withdrawn when threatened by Soviet advances and eventually destroyed by the Germans to prevent capture in 1945 and later scrapped. Three gigantic shells are all that survive, at the Imperial War Museum in London, the United States Army Ordinance Museum in Aberdeen, Maryland, and at the Polish Army Museum in Warsaw.

The wreckage of *Dora* at Grafenwöhr and *Gustav* north of Auerbach – by US and Soviet troops respectively.

The *Schwerer Gustav* program sums up in microcosm the unrealistic nature of Nazi weapons' procurement. To spend as much as they did on two enormous siege guns with the purpose of defeating the Maginot Line head on, and then miss the battle the weapon was intended for, use them once, ineffectively, before ultimately destroying them was wasteful of manpower and resources.

Left: *Germany fielded the largest railroad guns—in fact, the largest land artillery pieces—of all time. Only one vehicle was used once in combat firing just less than fifty projectiles against Sebastopol in 1942. All missed their primary targets.*

Right: *Model of Krupp 80cm* Schwerer Gustav, *a temporary exhibition at the Railway Museum in Utrecht. Note the double line of railtrack needed.*

French and Italian 15-inch Naval Guns

ITALIAN 15-INCH GUN

20th century
Italy
Makers: Ansaldo; Odero-Terni-Orlando
Location: none extant

Length: 64ft 11in
Weight: 109.9 tons
Caliber: 15 inches
Max range: 26.2 miles

In June 1940 when France was being overrun and Italy entered the war as an Axis power, both nations had battleships armed with 15-inch guns completed or under construction. Already in 1938 France had commissioned the two 26,500-ton "Dunkerque" class battleships armed with 330mm (13-inch) guns as a response to the German "Deutschland" class, and subsequently laid down two 15-inch armed battleships as a reply to Italy's similar vessels laid down in 1934. The new ships were the *Richelieu* and *Jean Bart*, each to be armed with eight 380mm (15-inch)/45-cal guns unusually arranged in two quadruple turrets mounted forward of the bridge superstructure. As originally designed these guns fired a 1,949lb AP shell to a maximum range of 45,600yd at thirty-five degrees of elevation. However, both ships had a checkered history, and when *Richelieu* was refitted in America in 1943 her guns were rebored to accept standard British 15-inch shells fired with a reduced charge so that maximum range fell to 41,065yd. *Jean Bart* was not completed until after the war and used guns intended for the *Clemenceau*, a projected third ship of the class whose incomplete hull was destroyed in 1944.

Between 1933 and 1940 the Italian Navy completed an extensive modernization of its four "Cavour" and "Duilio" class battleships dating from World War I. As well as lengthening the hulls and installing new more powerful machinery, the main armament was upgraded by the expedient of converting the existing 305mm (12-inch) guns to 320mm (12.6-inch). The modified weapons fired a heavier 1,157lb AP shell to a range of 32,150yd at a thirty-degree elevation compared to a 997lb shell to a range of 26,240yd at twenty degrees (the maximum possible in the original 12-inch mountings). In 1934 Italy laid down two "Vittorio Veneto" class battleships which would each be armed with nine 381mm (15-inch)/50-cal M1934 guns. These were completed in 1940 and although a further pair was laid down in 1938 only one (*Roma*) was ever completed. This 15-inch gun compared well with other contemporary weapons of the same caliber, firing a 1,951lb AP shell to range of 46,216yd at thirty-five degrees of elevation. Rate of fire was two rounds every 90 seconds.

Above Left: *The ultimate Italian battleships were the three 35,000-ton "Vittorio Veneto" class (name ship shown here) completed 1940–1942 and armed with nine 15-inch/50-cal guns in triple turrets. Significantly, the last to complete,* Roma, *was sunk by a German SD1400-X glider bomb on September 9, 1943—an indication of future trends in naval warfare and yet another nail in the coffin of the heavy naval gun.*

Below Left: *In the 1930s the Italian Navy modernized its four "Cavour" and "Duilio" class battleships dating from World War I and their 12-inch/305mm guns were modified to 12.4in/320mm caliber. This post war view shows the* Andrea Doria *with her ten 12.4in guns trained out to port.*

Above: *A close-up view of the forward quadruple 15-inch turret aboard the* Richelieu. *Internally the turret was split in half by a steel bulkhead and each of the resulting pairs of guns was served by its own shell room and magazine.*

Right: *The* Richelieu *was one of two French battleships laid down prior to World War II, although sister ship* Jean Bart *was not completed until 1949. These ships carried their main armament of eight 15-inch guns in a unique arrangement of two quadruple turrets both positioned forward of the superstructure.*

1941: US Navy 16-inch Mk. 6 and (1943) Mk. 7 Guns

16-INCH MK.7 GUN

20th Century
United States
Designer: Bureau of Ordnance

Barrel length: 66ft 10in
Weight: 134 tons
Caliber: 16 inch (406mm)
Max range: 24 miles

The US 16-inch Mk. 1 was produced at the end of World War I to arm the four "Maryland" class battleships (one of which was subsequently canceled) which each carried eights guns in four twin turrets. This 45-cal weapon fired a 2,100lb shell to a range of 35,000yd at thirty degrees of elevation. When battleship construction resumed in 1937 the lighter Mk. 6 16-inch/45-cal gun was selected for the two "North Carolina" class and five subsequent "South Dakota" class. This was of slightly lighter construction and fired a 2,700lb shell out to a range of 36,900yd at forty-five degrees elevation. Finally the four "Iowa" class battleships received the Mk. 7 16-inch/50-cal gun which fired the same shell to 42,345yd (still less than that achieved by the Japanese 18-inch guns). All of the new fast battleships carried nine 16-inch guns in three triple mountings although the projected "Montana" class (canceled in 1943) would have had an addition triple mounting. During World War II the US battleships fired their main armament almost exclusively in the shore bombardment role but in the naval battle of Guadalcanal (November 1942) the South Dakota class USS *Washington* engaged and seriously damaged the Japanese battleship *Hiei* which was left in a sinking condition before being finished off by air attack.

Right: *The after triple 16-inch turret aboard USS* Alabama. *Note the quad 40mm AA mounting on the turret roof.*

Opposite: *Between 1937 and 1945 the United States laid down and completed no fewer than ten fast battleships, all armed with nine 16-inch guns in three triple mountings. These are the forward turrets of the USS* Alabama *(BB60) now preserved as a memorial museum at Mobile in its name state.*

1942: Japanese Navy 460mm Guns

460MM GUN

20th Century
Japan
Designer: Captain Kikuo Fujimoto

Length: 69ft 5in
Weight: 162 tons
Caliber: 460mm (18.11 inches)
Max range: 26 miles

At 68,000 tons displacement the two "Yamato" class were, by a very large margin, the largest battleships ever built. They were also the most heavily armed with nine 18-inch guns in three triple turrets, which were the heaviest caliber ever mounted in battleships of any nation (although note the British 18-inch gun described in Chapter 2). Developed in the 1930s, both the ships and their guns were built and manufactured in great secrecy, the guns being referred to as the 400mm (16-inch) Type 94 and it was not until the end of the war the Americans realized the true size of these weapons. A total of twenty-seven of these guns were produced, a figure which included some for a third ship (*Shinano*) which was subsequently completed as an aircraft carrier.

The new guns were actually 460mm weapons which equated to 18.11-inch Imperial measurement. Each gun had an overall length of just over 69ft, weighed 162 tons, and fired either a 3,219lb AP or a 2,998lb common shell to a maximum range of 45,960yd. The propellant charge is variously given as 728lb or 794lb. The total rotating mass of the turret with its three guns was 2,470 tons—equivalent to a typical fully laden World War II destroyer! Also available was a shrapnel fragmentation shell which was intended for anti-aircraft use, the guns being capable of elevating to forty-five degrees. Aboard the "Yamato" class battleships stowage was provided for 100 rounds per gun and rate of fire was almost exactly two rounds per minute, reducing to three rounds every two minutes at the highest angles of elevation—a relatively high rate of fire for such large weapons. As both ships were sunk before the end of the war, the available data is mostly taken from investigation of a trial mounting found ashore after the end of hostilities.

Right: *The Japanese battleship* Yamato, *and her sister* Musashi, *were the largest and most powerfully armed of their kind ever built.*

Left: *A close up view of the after triple 18-inch turret aboard the* Yamato *while she was fitting out in September 1941. Note the high angle of elevation of one of the guns. In the background is one of the ship's four triple 6-inch/155mm mountings.*

Below Left: *Despite their immense power,* Yamato *and* Musashi *never had an opportunity to use their 18-inch guns against an enemy battleship and the fact that both were sunk by air attack in the closing stages of the Pacific War served to illustrate how aircraft carriers were now the new capital ships. This image shows* Yamato *under attack by aircraft of Task Force 58 on April 7, 1945, and she sank several hours later after numerous bomb and torpedo hits.*

1944 US 240mm M1 Howitzer

240MM M1 HOWITZER

20th Century
United States
Location: Various Taiwanese islands
Designer: Bureau of Ordnance

Barrel length: 27ft 6in
Weight: 64,700lb
Caliber: 240mm (9.4 inches)
Max range: 14.3 miles
Max range: 13,000 yards

The 240mm M1 Howitzer, nicknamed the "Black Dragon," was the largest caliber artillery piece fielded by the United States in World War II and continued in use until after the Korean War of 1950–1953. A bunker-buster adept at destroying reinforced concrete positions and bridges at long range, the M1 began development in 1941 and first saw action in January 1944 with the US Fifth Army at the Anzio Beachhead in Italy, where it was successfully used in counter-battery fire against German heavy artillery. It went on to see action in the Pacific and in rest of Europe, becoming famous for its accuracy and power.

A self-propelled version was tested mounting an M1 on a heavy tank chassis, but this hadn't got beyond the prototype stage before World War II ended. The M1 weighed had an L/35 barrel 27.5ft long that fired HE 360lb shells to a range of 14.3 miles. Towed in two parts by 20mph 38-ton tractors, an M1 typically took eight hours to assemble with a truck crane and was operated by a crew of fourteen. A few M1s are apparently still in service today as coastal defense with the Taiwanese Army on their frontline islands with mainland China.

Far Left: *Rear view of a 240mm howitzer at the US Army Field Artillery Museum, Ft. Sill, OK*

Above and Below Left: *The M1 tube was transported separately behind various prime movers—M35, M6 HST, M33—and then had to be craned onto its carriage for firing.*

Right: *Front view of 240mm howitzer of Battery B, 697th Field Artillery Battalion, just before firing.*

US Navy 16-inch Guns Loading and Firing

This series of images aboard a typical World War II US Navy battleship armed with 16-inch guns in triple turrets shows the sequence of operations to raise shells and powder charges from the magazines, transport them to the turrets and load them into the guns. It also shows some of the activity associated with aiming and firing the guns. *All images via NARA*

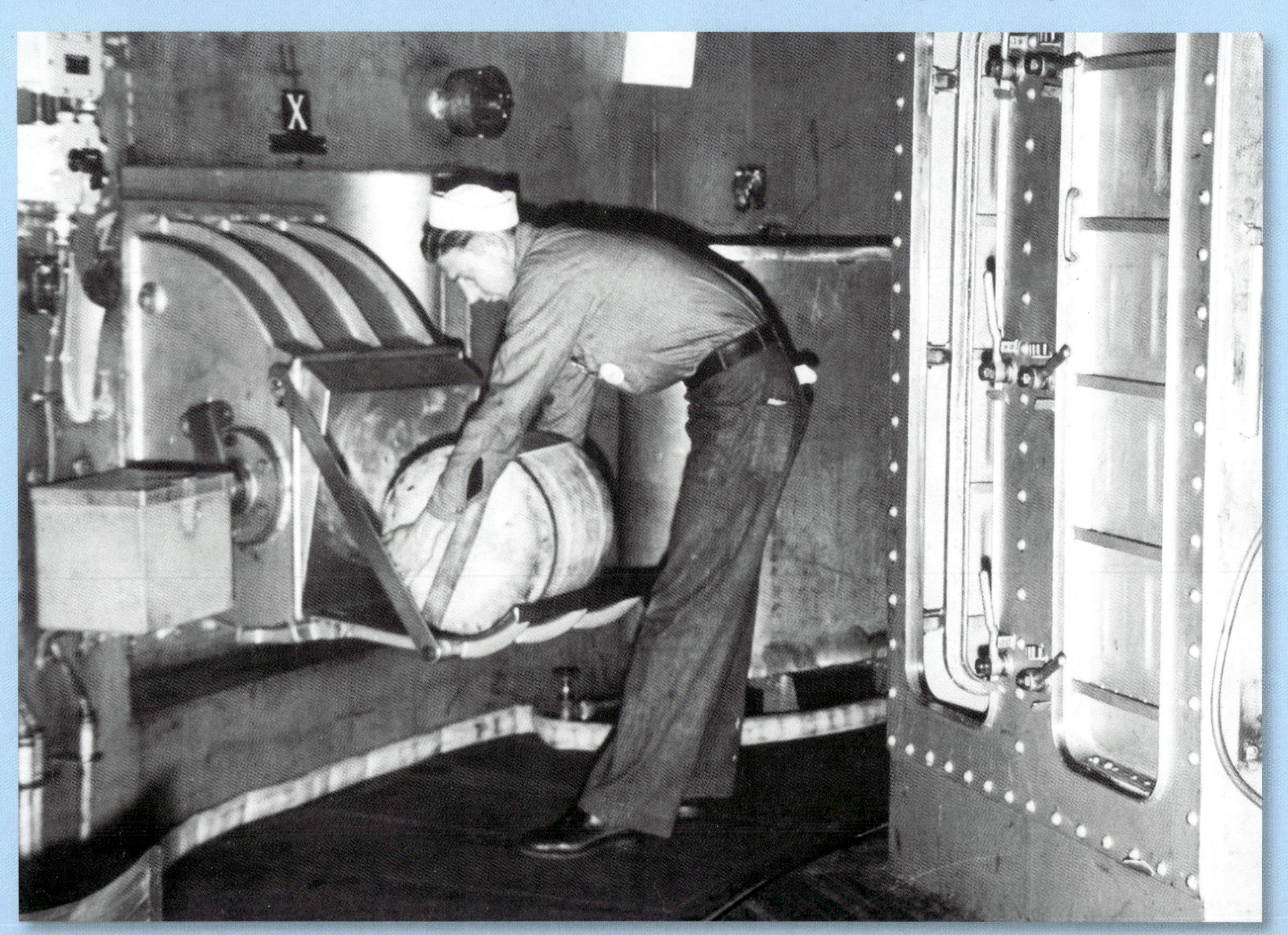

Right: *The propellant powder charges were held in magazines at the lowest level in the ship which could be quickly flooded in the event of a fire or explosion. Each bagged charge was passed to the powder handling room through a flashproof scuttle.*

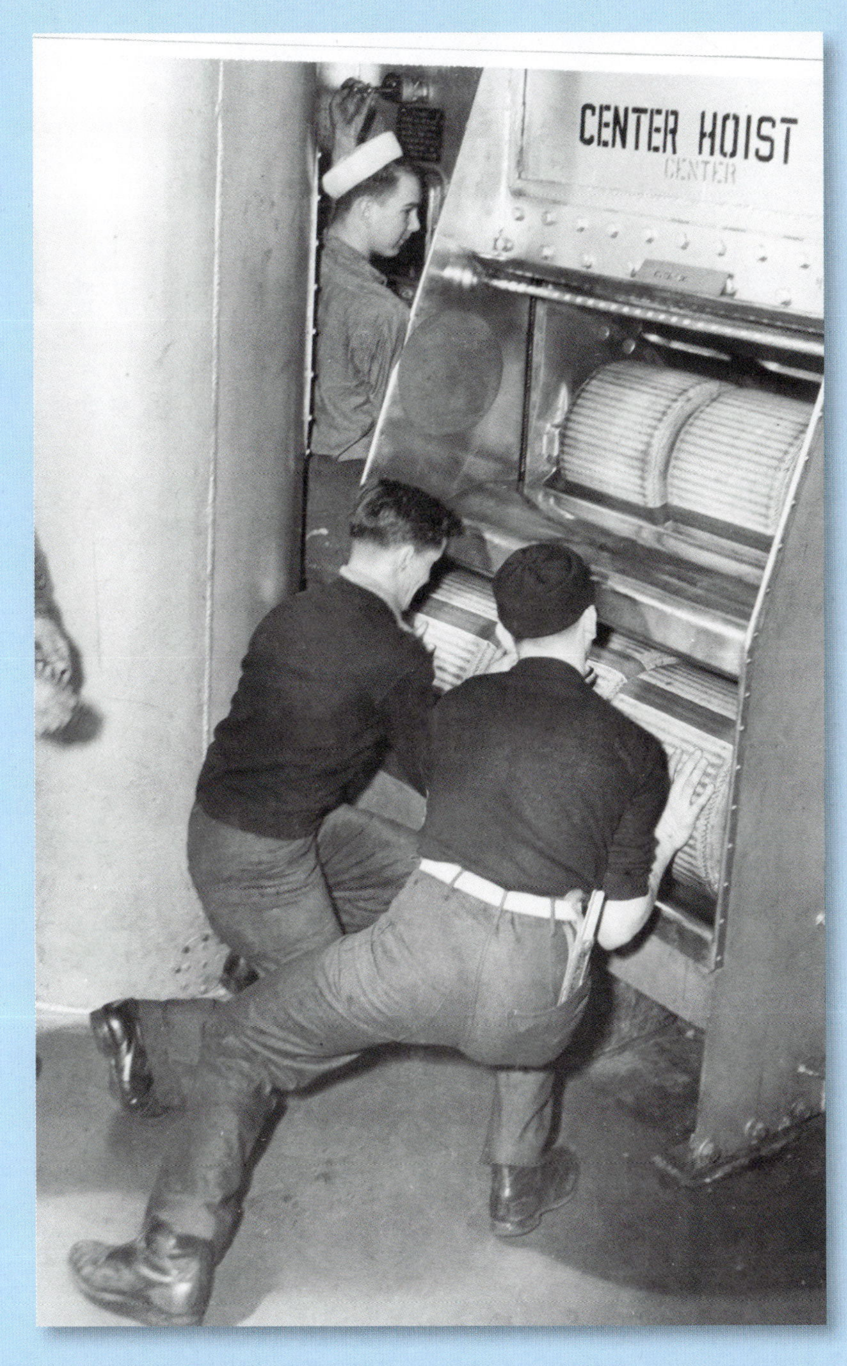

Far Left: *Each charge weighed around 90lb and six were needed for each gun. Here they are placed in two trays each containing three charges. The trays are then hoisted up to the guns when required. As a safety precaution flashproof doors at the bottom and top of the hoist cannot both be open at the same time.*

Left: *The 16-inch shells, each weighing around 1,900lb are stored in the shell rooms one deck above the magazines. From there they are moved into fixed storage racks around the inside of the armored barbette and as required are maneuvered onto a central platform which rotates with the turret.*

TURRET
ONE

Far Left: *In turn each shell is fed nose uppermost into the shell hoist which takes it up to a position immediately behind the gun loading tray.*

Left: *At the gun the shell is tipped forward into the loading tray and rammed into the breech. The rammer and both shell and powder hoists were electrically driven.*

Right: *With the shell loaded, the gun crew wait for the charges to be tipped out onto the loading tray from the adjacent powder hoist. Note that the door is open so that the one at the bottom of the hoist will be closed.*

Left: *As the charges are tipped onto the loading tray, they are rammed forward, the tray withdrawn and the breech closed.*

Below: *Some turrets were equipped with a stereoscopic rangefinder whose sighting arms could be seen projecting each side of the turret rear. Ranges obtained could be used to direct the turret in local control if necessary.*

Right: *The loading process is closely monitored from turret control housed in a separate compartment at the rear of the turret. The cylindrical structure on the right is part of the rangefinder assembly.*

Left: *Aiming and firing the guns was normally controlled and directed from the Director Tower high up in the ships superstructure. Information and date from this as well as the turret's rangefinders and other sighting sources was passed to the Plotting Room (shown here) situated below the armored deck. Here operators can feed in data such as range, course and speed of the target to an electrically driven analog computer which calculates the necessary aiming instructions for the guns.*

Right: *Despite the enormous power of a battleship's guns, their firing is actuated by a simple trigger action. The operator, on instructions from the director, can set the guns to fire broadsides or salvoes. When he presses the trigger it completes the firing circuit but the guns will not discharge until the ship passes a predetermined point in pitch and roll in order to achieve consistent results.*

Far Right: *Shoot! USS* Iowa *fires a salvo from her aft turret. Already the next shells and charges will be moving up the hoists ready for loading as the cycle continues.*

Chapter 5: The Atomic Age

Opposite: *During the Cold War, the US and NATO were outnumbered in Central Europe and faced 50,000 Soviet tanks. The end of World War II by use of the atomic bomb introduced the idea of tactical atomic weapons—the sort of thing that could be fired by artillery. Trouble was that at that stage nuclear weapons were big (the bomb dropped on Hiroshima weighed 9,700lb) and the US's largest mobile artillery piece was the Black Dragon (see pp. 192–193). It could fire a 360lb shell 25,000yd—just not powerful enough. That's when "Atomic Annie" came along, but missile development rendered this form of munitions' delivery unnecessary. (See pp. 210–212.)*

The end of World War II saw the beginning of the nuclear age. The atomic bomb had become the latest superweapon and one which could undoubtedly deliver on everything an ultimate weapon should. Its proliferation has made the world a much more dangerous place, with the prospect of even worse to come—whether by design or accident. Besides the increase in the number of nuclear weapon states any mistake or natural disaster in a nation with civil nuclear power invariably has the same kind of effect as a war weapon and weapons-grade material can also be made while masked by civil nuclear program.

In 1945 at the end of the hostilities most of the developed world divided into two main rival western and eastern power blocs led by the US and the USSR, with their respective international military organizations, NATO and the Warsaw Pact. Mutually antagonistic political differences inspired violent posturing and paranoia which spurred on yet another furious arms race. Soon both sides had more than enough atomic ordnance to guarantee MAD—mutually assured destruction—and except for a few dangerous moments such as the 1962 Cuban Missile Crisis what became known as the Cold War developed. All-out armageddon was avoided and instead the two blocs fought for power and influence across the world in a simmering game of politico-military chess that saw several proxy wars erupt, all of which were fought with conventional weapons. Some of these local conflicts between individual states, tribal and civil wars or struggles for liberation from colonial occupation were just happening anyway and each bloc chose a side to back along political, commercial or just pragmatic lines. The world was awash with weapons created by the rival military-industrial complexes of this Cold War. Despite the background threat of multiple-warhead ICBMs (inter continental ballistic missile) capable of being launched by land, sea, and air systems, the development of non-nuclear weapons continued unabated. Heavyweight superguns had a final postwar flowering before artillery retrenched as a powerful tactical battlefield asset as opposed to some long-range strategic threat—a role now taken by missiles and air power. As usual these final superguns were pushing the boundaries of what was possible in terms of weight, size and transportability. Both US and USSR produced various self-propelled weapons to bombard an enemy's deep areas of logistics and supply, but also with the idea of battlefield use of tactical nuclear weapons which now seems a pretty daft idea given their relatively short ranges. However, they were still cumbersome, their crews were almost completely unprotected, they were vulnerable to aircraft and required a convoy of vehicles to keep them supplied. A few such as the 1961 8-inch (203mm) SP M110 Howitzer sold worldwide and were a success, but most didn't get beyond the trials stage.

In the final attempts (so far) to build monster guns a Canadian named Gerald Bull must be mentioned. Beginning

Above: *On January 31, 2008, a 7lb projectile was fired at 10.64MJ (megajoules) with a muzzle velocity of 8,268ft/sec using electromagnetic railgun (EMRG) technology. This is one of the two electromagnetic railgun prototypes on display aboard the joint high speed vessel USS* Millinocket *(JHSV 3) in port at Naval Base San Diego.*

in 1961 with US/Canada Project HARP (High Altitude Research Project) Bull was part of a team that built a test gun using an old US 16-inch (410mm) 50-caliber naval gun that was re-bored to 100 caliber in his quest to deliver payloads into space. With the collapse of that project Bull eventually began Project Babylon—an attempt to build the world's biggest gun for the Iraqi dictator Saddam Hussein, which ended with an embargo on the western manufactured parts and Bull's assassination by persons unknown. With his death went the idea of an enormous gun that could fire into space.

Modern artillery is, above all, mobile—towed or self-propelled—and is still divided along the classic lines of gun, howitzer, and mortar, along with the reintroduction of rocket artillery. Its most important aspect is in the use of indirect fire, but until now indirect fire meant area fire and suppression—accurate enough to target a grid square on a map but not a specific location such as a single bunker or vehicle. In the late 1970s precision munitions started to appear which followed a laser designation that identified the target precisely. Shells are stabilized with rifled spin using a rotating driving band of soft metal near the base of the shell to line it up with the rifling of the barrel or else fin-stabilized for smoothbore mortar weapons that reduce wear, enable longer ranges, and are cheaper to produce. The propellants that fire the shells have evolved into three main types: single, double or triple with different mixes of nitrocellulose, nitroglycerin, and nitroguanidine, again tailored to purpose for specific targets. Some artillery uses metal shell cases that include both the round and the propellant which simplifies and speeds up loading. Bagged propellant allows more flexibility, the amount dependent on the range to the target, and makes the handling of larger shells easier. Cheap solid-state electronic multifunction fuses started to appear around 1980 and soon became standard. With these refinements and technological advances increased TOT (time on target) and MRSI (multiple rounds simultaneous impact) became possible—giving no warning of arrival and so especially devastating to targets caught in the open.

The increases in mobility and explosive power of modern weapons and the acceleration of communications have speeded up the battlespace, making it an even more dangerous place than battlefields of old. All-arms combat requires all the different arms—and the technical ability to coordinate them. The dominance of armor has been challenged by missiles from air assets and individual soldiers with hand-held wire guided or rocket propelled munitions, but tanks are still vital—and required in symmetrical wars against similar opponents. Asymmetric warfare calls for a different mix of assets. In the most recent asymmetric wars successful combat and casualties have been as a result of the use of automated robotic elements—IEDs (improvised explosive device) triggered by pressure (like mines) or set off by an observer phone signal and drones guided by a pilot thousands of miles away using equipment similar to shoot-em-up computer games and virtual reality. The age of the supergun seems to have passed and superweapons now have wings or fins with no need to be shot from a barrel. Perhaps energy weapons such as the developing electromagnetic pulse US Railgun will revive it.

Above: *On September 11, 1944, the first V–2 rocket was launched from a forest just outside Gouvy, Belgium. While the V–2's military results were minimal, the effect of the weapons on morale was considerable. It would not be long before long-range and then inter-continental missiles were developed.*

Naval Weapons

Below: *The last battleship armed with heavy guns ever to be completed and commissioned was the French Navy's* Jean Bart *which carried eight 15-inch guns in two quadruple turrets.*

Opposite: *The US Navy's "Iowa" class battleships had active careers after World War II. Here USS* New Jersey *fires her 16-inch guns in support of United Nations forces at Wonsan just after the outbreak of the Korean War in July 1951.*

By 1945 the battleship had been consigned to secondary duties, its place as the arbiter of seapower being taken by the aircraft carrier, whose squadrons could deliver heavy ordnance in the form of bombs and torpedoes over distances measured in hundreds of miles instead of the 20–25 miles achievable by the ship's heavy guns. No more battleships were laid down after World War II and many projected or under construction were canceled. Notable exceptions were the French *Jean Bart* which was launched in 1940 but was laid up during the war and only completed in 1949, and the British HMS *Vanguard* completed in 1946 armed with 15-inch guns dating back to World War I that had been removed from the battlecruisers *Courageous* and *Glorious* when they were converted to aircraft carriers in the 1920s. Both battleships were decommissioned in the early 1960s. In contrast the US Navy retained the four "Iowa" class battleships completed during World War II and these were used to provide naval gunfire support to US troops in Korea and Vietnam. During the 1980s they were modified to carry Harpoon anti-ship and Tomahawk land-attack missiles and in 1991 USS *Missouri* and USS *Wisconsin* launched missile attacks against Iraqi targets during Operation Desert Storm. After that they were laid up and the last pair were stricken from the Navy Register in 2006. Currently all four "Iowa" class as well as several older battleships are preserved as museum ships—a sad contrast to Britain which was once the world's leading naval power but has no preserved a single battleship from either of the world wars.

Although the naval heavy gun was rapidly discarded after 1945, there were many developments affecting medium calibers. The US Navy developed an automatic 8-inch gun which armed three "Des Moines" class heavy cruisers completed in 1948–1949 and both they and the Royal Navy also commissioned light cruisers armed with automatic 6-inch guns. Today medium-caliber guns ranging from 100mm to 130mm arm most frigates and destroyers, heavier and longer-range hitting power being provided by new generations of guided missiles. However, during the 1990s work began on extended-range munitions using rocket assistance which could be fired from the standard 5-inch gun and offered ranges up to 60 nautical miles. Technical difficulties led to this program being terminated but subsequently the 155mm/62-cal Advanced Gunnery System was developed for the USS *Zumwalt* (DDG1000) which commissioned in 2016. This would have fired the Long Range Land Attack Projectile (LRLAP), a rocket assisted projectile with GPS/INS guidance, capable of accurately hitting targets at ranges up to 100 nautical miles but this has now been canceled on cost grounds.

1945: US 36-inch *Little David* Mortar

36-INCH MORTAR

20th Century
United States
Designer: US Army
Location: Aberdeen Proving Ground, Maryland, USA

Barrel length: 22 feet
Weight: 40 tons
Caliber: 36 inches (914mm)
Max range: 6 miles

Having something of the ancient bombard in its appearance, the *Little David* Mortar—along with the British Mallet's Mortar (see p. 78)—is the largest gun by caliber ever made. Originally built at the US Army's Aberdeen Proving Ground in Maryland as a fixed test gun to research aerial bombs, like the British weapon it never saw combat or got beyond the test-firing stage. However, in 1944 when the US was considering the invasion of Japan and looking for fortification-busting weapons, *Little David* was converted to be transportable in two sections by two artillery M26A1 tank tractors accompanied by a bulldozer to prepare its firing platform and a crane to help in assembly, which took about twelve hours. When Japan surrendered following two air-delivered atomic bomb strikes the invasion was canceled and the project was abandoned.

Little David has survived and can still be seen at the Aberdeen Proving Ground. It is really just a huge barrel that was embedded in an underground steel box and looked exactly like a scaled-up version of the standard-issue close-quarter weapon, but was lowered flat to the ground in order to be muzzle-loaded. *Little David* had a caliber of 36 inches (914mm) firing 3,650lb shells up to a range of six miles.

Above: *Shell from* Little David*, at the museum.*

Far Left and Right: Little David *under test at the Aberdeen Proving Ground. One of the largest-caliber artillery pieces ever produced—although by weight of round, the German* Dora *fired a heavier shell—it had a limited range and its accuracy wasn't good.*

Left: Little David *at the US Army Ordnance Museum (Aberdeen Proving Ground, MD) today. The mortar traveled separately from the box containing the elevation, traverse, and other control mechanisms*

1953: US M65 Atomic Cannon

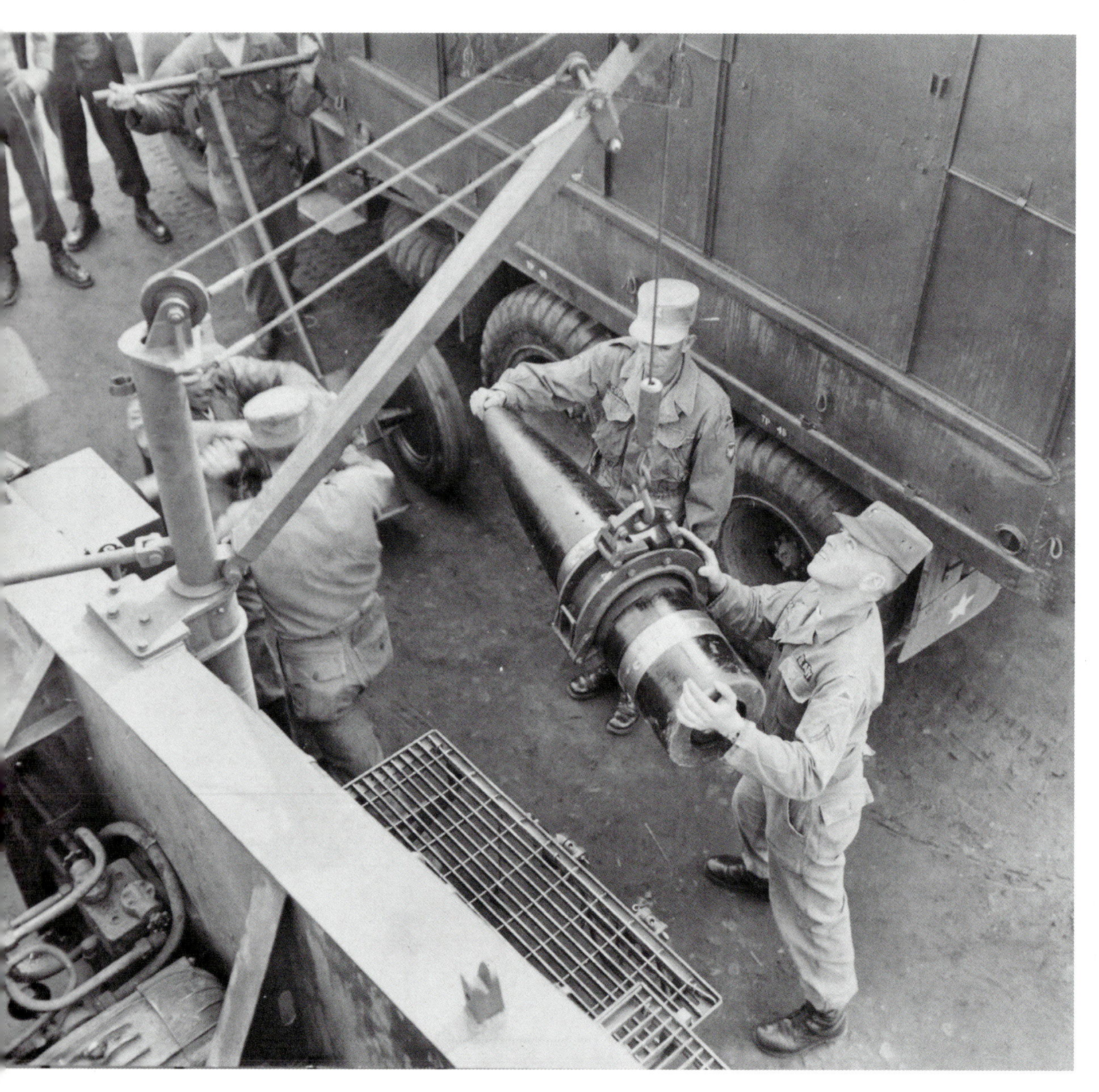

On January 20, 1953, Dwight D. Eisenhower became President of the United States. In the inaugural parade there was one considerable show of strength: an M65 "Atomic Annie" Cannon.

The US M65 Atomic Cannon was a Cold War weapon built to fire nuclear munitions. It began development in 1949 using existing equipment as a starting point—the United States' 240mm (9.5-inch) shell and the German K5 (E) railway gun—but by 1953 it had morphed into a towed artillery piece using two custom-built trucks. It was also successfully tested that year and fired the only nuclear round it ever did—a 15kT W9 warhead to a range of seven miles. Following this some twenty units were made at the Watertown and Watervliet arsenals and deployed overseas to West Germany, Japan, and South Korea.

The seven-man crew took 15 minutes to prepare the M65 for firing using hydraulic jacks and winches. It could fire 600lb HE T-124 projectiles or the 15 kt W9 nuclear warhead to a maximum range of about thirty miles.

Given the accelerated weapons' development of the Cold War, the M65 was rendered obsolete almost immediately by other US nuclear artillery —the 6-inch (155mm) and the 8-inch (203mm)—and missile and rocket technology. However, being a prestige weapon that reassured its NATO allies in Europe, the United States kept it in service until the early 1960s. Over half a dozen M65s survive today and can be seen at various locations in US including the US Army Ordnance Museum, Aberdeen MD and Watervliet Arsenal Museum, NY.

This Spread: *On May 25, 1953, the Atomic Cannon was fired and detonated a 15kT W9 warhead at the Nevada test site under the codename "Grable"—the only nuclear warhead ever fired from an artillery piece. As the Korean War continued, the rumor that an atomic cannon able to fire a 15kT W9 nuclear warhead might be deployed on the Korean Peninsula helped usher in the end of the war.*

This Page: *A battery of "Atomic Annies." Note the shell at bottom right.*

M65 ATOMIC CANNON

20th Century
United States
Maker: Watertown and Watervliet arsenals
Locations: US Army Ordnance Museum, Maryland; Watervliet Arsenal Museum, New York.

Length: 84 feet
Weight: 83.3 tons
Caliber: 11 inches (280mm)
Max range: 30 miles

1956: USSR 2A3 Kondensator 2P 406mm SP Howitzer

The USSR's 406mm 2A3 Kondensator 2P self-propelled howitzer was another superheavy artillery piece that was developed during the Cold War in response to similar US developments and deployments. The gun and its self-propelling carrier were designed separately and unified at the Kirov Works in Leningrad. The 2A3 Kondensator 2P's SM-54 gun fired HE and nuclear projectiles weighing 1,257lb, up to maximum range of sixteen 16 miles and was operated by a crew of eight. It was powered by a 750hp 12-6B diesel engine. Various problems of recoil damage to the gun and its carriage were solved, but the weapon was cumbersome, difficult to transport and had a slow rate of fire. In the end only four units were produced and after extensive testing had a very short service life, held in an artillery reserve without ever being deployed. Perhaps its most auspicious moment was the impression its huge size made on Western observers during a 1957 parade in Red Square. As with other massive guns of this period their time had passed and they were being replaced by new sophisticated missile technology. Today a 2A3 Kondensator 2P can be seen at the Central Museum of Armed Forces, Moscow, Russia.

Below: *2A3 Kondensator 2P in the Central Museum of the Armed Forces (Moscow).*

2A3 KONDENSATOR 2P 406MM SP HOWITZER

20th Century
Soviet Union
Maker: Kirov Works, Leningrad
Location: Central Museum of Armed Forces, Moscow, Russia

Length: 65ft 7in
Weight: 64 tons
Caliber: 16 inch (406mm)
Max range: 16 miles
Ordnance: shells
Max range: 13,000 yards

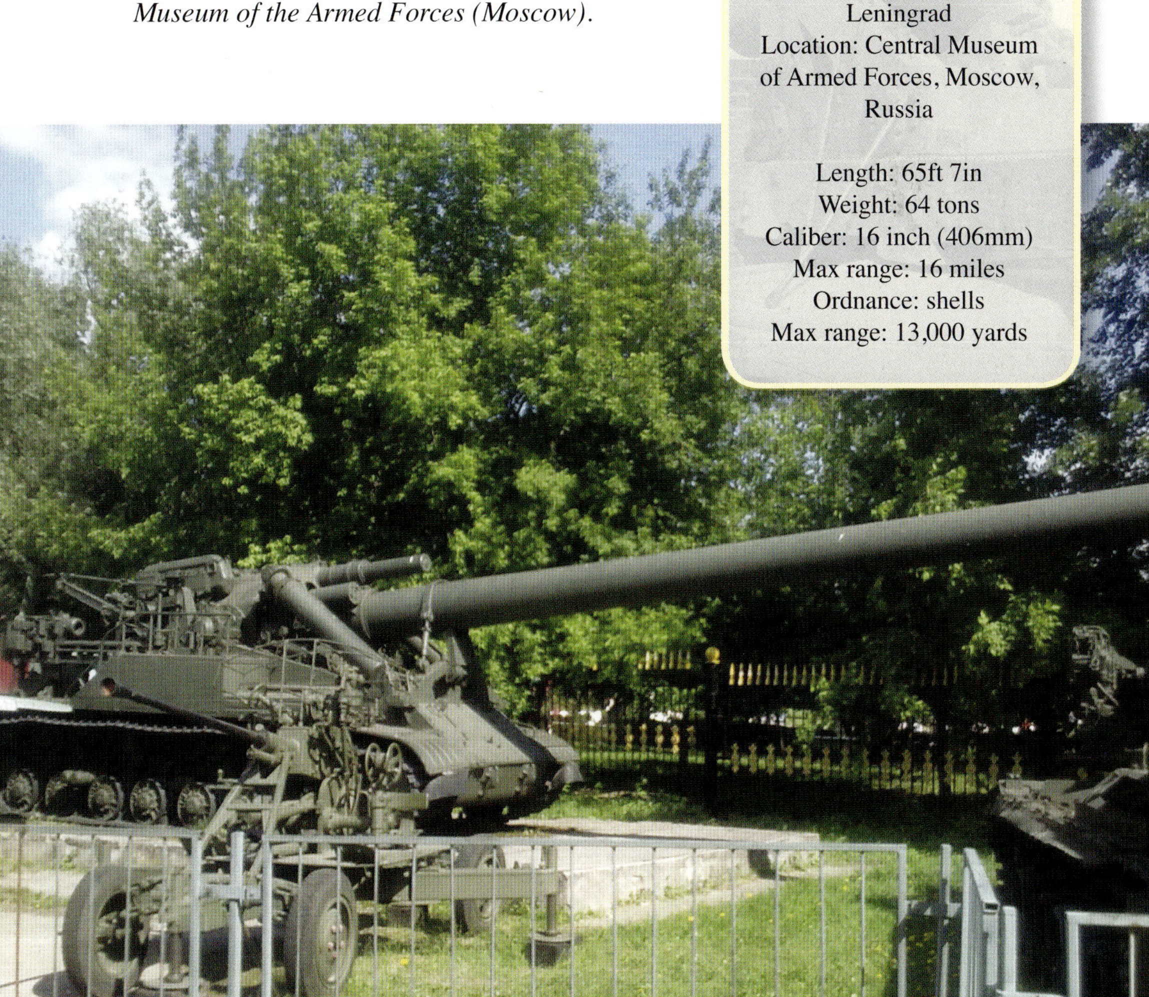

1957: USSR 2B1 Oka 420mm SP Gun

The USSR's 2B1 Oka was an experimental weapon whose design flaws ensured that it didn't get beyond the test-firing stage. It was built at the Kirov Plant in St. Petersburg, and was a huge gun mounted centrally on a mobile firing platform with eight double-tired road wheels heavily strutted to counter both the weight and the recoil. Its 420mm (17-inch) gun had a colossal long smoothbore barrel that fired 1,654lb shells to a maximum range of twenty-eight miles, and was operated by a crew of seven men. It was powered by a V12-5 diesel engine, but the sheer length of its barrel made transport very difficult and the blast recoil was too strong for the mounting carriage to contain, consistently damaging various components, while the engine struggled to cope with so much weight. The massive size of its shells precluded any sustained rate of fire and like its American counterparts the M110 SP howitzer and M107 SP 175mm gun the Soviet 2B1 Oka offered no protection to its crew. Its development continued until the early 1960s, when the concept of such superguns was finally abandoned by both sides with the arrival of ballistic missile technology.

Right and Opposite: *The 420mm 2B1 Oka and one of the shells it fired, seen at the Saint-Petersburg Artillery Museum.*

2B1 OKA 240MM SP GUN

20th Century
Soviet Union
Maker: Kirov Plant, St Petersburg
Location: St Petersburg Artillery Museum, Russia

Barrel length: 65ft 7in
Weight: 55.3 tons
Caliber: 17 inch (420mm)
Max range: 28 miles

1961: US 203mm (8-inch) SP M110 Howitzer

The M110 began development in the mid-1950s, the 203mm gun being based on the British 8-inch howitzer that the United States Army had used in World War II. The tracked chassis was the same as that used by the US M107 SP 175mm gun. Indeed, both the M110 and the M107 were modular and parts were easily interchangeable with each other for armies that deployed both weapons. Entering service in 1961, for a while the M110 was the largest artillery piece in the US Army, used in the Vietnam War and both Gulf Wars (Desert Shield and Desert Storm). It was also exported to many other countries including Egypt, Greece, Japan, Morocco, Pakistan, South Korea, Spain, Taiwan, and Turkey.

The M110 sported the M2A2 L/25 8-inch (203mm) gun that fired HE-FRAG shells weighing 204lb to a range of 10.5–18 miles. It could also fire nuclear projectiles and had a loading assist system and a crew of five men, though room for only two rounds of ammunition, the rest being carried by accompanying M458 tracked cargo carriers. It is powered by a General Motors 405hp 8V71T diesel engine capable of 34mph with a range of 310 miles. Later versions include the 1971 M110A1 fitted with the longer-barreled M201 203mm L/37 howitzer that fires rocket-assisted cluster bombs and nuclear or chemical projectiles; the 1978 M110A2 fitted with a double muzzle break and an increase in range to 18 miles.

One criticism of the M110 is that it has no defensive protection or armament leaving its crew extremely vulnerable to counter-battery fire, snipers, and aircraft, however its record of service is excellent.

Left: *Preserved example at the US Army Field Artillery Museum, Fort Sill, OK.*

Below: *Only two of the large 203mm projectiles could be carried on the M110 vehicle, the rest of the ammunition supply was towed by a support vehicle. A dozer-type spade was fitted to the rear of the hull to counter the 203mm gun's violent recoil. The powered spade was raised from the ground and stowed when traveling—as can be seen at the back of this preserved example.*

Right: *M110A2 breech.*

203MM SP M110 HOWITZER

20th Century
United States
Maker: General Motor Corps
Location: US Army Field Artillery Museum, Fort Sill, OK

Length: 35ft
Weight: 28.35 tons
Caliber: 8 inch (203mm)
Max range: 18 miles

1961 Project HARP (High Altitude Research Project)

PROJECT HARP

20th Century
United States & Canada
Designer: Gerald Bull
Location: Barbados

Barrel length: 130ft
Weight: unknown
Caliber: 16-inch (410 mm)
Max range: 112 miles

This gun is still visible in Barbados. It was transported overland via a purpose-built railway that is no longer extant.

The joint US and Canadian High Altitude Research Project was the brainchild of Gerald Bull, a charismatic and controversial Canadian ballistics engineer who was convinced he could design a supergun capable of firing satellites into space. At first his funded research coincided with interest from both the Canadian and American governments with the gun used as a money-saving option to test ICBM re-entry vehicles. An old US 16-inch (410mm) 50-caliber naval gun was provided and later rebored to 100-caliber. The first test firings were carried out in Barbados and the last in Yuma, AZ. On November 18, 1966, at Yuma a 400lb Martlet 2 projectile was fired briefly into space, setting an altitude record of 110 miles that still stands today. However, the program was terminated due to differences between the two governments and Bull was left to carry on by himself. During the project various versions of the Martlet test projectiles were made. In 1962 Martlet 1 weighed 450lb, was 6.6 inches in diameter and 70 inches in length. Only four were manufactured and two were test-fired. Martlet 2 was the most used version using various weights and configurations with about 200 being manufactured and fired. Martlet 3 was a rocket-propelled projectile built and tested but found unsuccessful. Other versions were proposed but never built before the project ended. By the time the program ended about 1,000 firings had taken place, and the data collected during the HARP project represents half of all the upper-atmospheric data ever collected.

1988: Iraq Project Babylon Supergun "Baby Babylon" and "Big Babylon"

Left: *Part of the Iraqi supergun "Project Babylon" behind the British 3.7-inch Anti-Aircraft Gun Mk. II of 1943 in foreground.*

Gerald Bull didn't give up on his supergun idea of firing satellites into space. For a while he had to find work designing other weapons, but in 1988 he was headhunted by the Iraqi dictator Saddam Hussein, who was also interested in the idea of a massive long-range artillery weapon to support his designs on neighboring countries.

The first of the guns Bull built, "Baby Babylon," was a prototype purely for testing. The second, "Big Babylon," was designed to be considerably larger than the first and was the space gun Bull had always wanted to build to send satellites into orbit. Other superlarge cannon were planned, one with a barrel length of 100ft, a bore of 350mm (13.8 inches) and a range of 625 miles; another with a barrel length of about 200ft and a bore of 23.6 inches.

Specialist metal firms in Canada, Britain, Germany, France, Spain, and Italy had all begun to manufacture various parts that had been disguised by Bull and the Iraqis spreading their orders, however such prospective weapons would bring both Iran and Israel within range and in March 1990 Gerald Bull was assassinated near his home in Belgium. After the 1991 Gulf Wardefeat the Iraqis admitted the existence of Project Babylon and the gun parts in Iraq were destroyed by UN inspectors.

Several parts of what would have been the Big Babylon barrel were intercepted by British customs and can be seen today at the Royal Artillery Museum in Woolwich, London.

BIG BABYLON

20th Century
Iraq
Designer: Gerald Bull
Location: some parts at Royal Artillery Museum, London, England

Barrel length: 512 feet
Weight: 1 ton
Caliber: 3.3 feet (1m)
Max range: unknown

1971: USSR 2S4 Tyulpan M-240 240mm SP Mortar

The Soviet 2S4 Tyulpan M-240 is a self-propelled 240mm (9.5-inch) breech-loading heavy mortar that was developed from the earlier M-240 towed version. It is the world's largest mortar in use today. Beginning development in the 1960s, it was issued to the army in 1971 and has seen service in Afghanistan and Chechenya, with claims that it has been seen in the Russian-backed breakaway Donetsk People's Republic and in Syria too. Some 400 were built.

It has a distinctive mode of deploying its main weapon to fire in that it is lowered on its base in front of its carriage by hydraulic pistons. The 2S4 Tyulpan's 240mm main armament fires 287lb shells to a range of 5.9–12 miles depending on which ammunition is used (HE, AP, chemical, or nuclear), the longer range being reached by rocket-assisted projectiles. There is also a laser-guided round for this weapon known as the *Smelchak* (Daredevil). It has a crew of five and can fire at the rate of one round a minute. It also has a 7.62mm machine gun mounted for self-defense fitted above the commander's cupola. It is powered by a 520hp V-59 diesel engine with a maximum speed of 38.5 mph and a range of 310 miles.

Left and Right: *240mm self-propelled mortar 2B8 (GRAU designation 2S4).*

2S4 TYULPAN M-240 SP MORTAR

20th Century
Soviet Union:
Location: still in service

Length: 21feet
Weight: 30 tons
Caliber: 9.5 inch (240mm)
Max range: 12 miles

Bibliography

Archibald, E.H.H.: *The Metal Fighting Ship in the Royal Navy, 1860–1970*; Blandford Press, 1971.

Archibald, E.H.H.: *The Wooden Ship in the Royal Navy AD897–1860*; Blandford Press, 1968.

Brown, D.K.: *Warrior to Dreadnought. Warship Development 1860–1905*; Chatham Publishing, 1977.

Field, Ron: *Fortress 38: American Civil War Fortifications (2) Land and Field Fortifications*; Osprey, 2003.

Hodges, Peter: *The Big Gun. Battleship Main Armament 1860-1945*; Conway Maritime Press, 1981.

Hogg, Ian V.: *German Artillery of World War Two*; Greenhill Books, 1977.

Hogg, Ian V.: *The Illustrated Encyclopedia of Artillery*; Quarto Books, 1987.

Katcher, Philip: *American Civil War Artillery 1861–1865*; Osprey, 2001.

Konstam, Angus: *Fortress 6: American Civil War Fortifications (1) Coastal brick and stone forts*; Osprey, 2003.

Lavery, Brian: *Nelson's Navy. The Ships, Men and Organisation 1793–1815*; Conway Maritime Press, 1989.

Lewis, Emanuel Raymond: *Seacoast Fortifications of the United States*; Pictorial Histories Publishing Company, 1990.

McGovern, Terrance C. & Berhow, Mark A.: *Fortress 4: American Coastal Defenses 1885–1950*; Osprey, 2006.

McGovern, Terrance & Smith, Bolling: *Fortress 44: American Coastal Defenses of Corregidor and Manila Bay 1898–1945*; Osprey, 2006.

Romanych, M. & Rupp, M.: *New Vanguard 205: 42cm "Big Bertha" and German Siege Artillery of World War I*; Osprey, 2013.

Silverstone, Paul H.: *Directory of the World's Capital Ships*; Ian Allan Ltd, 1984.

Zaloga, Steven J.: *New Vanguard 231: Railway Guns of World War II*; Osprey, 2016.

Photo Credits

1 Air Sea Media collection; 2–3 Simon Forty; 4–5, LOC, Alfred T. Palmer, photographer; 6–7 Artworld by Mark Franklin; 8 PHGCOM/WikiCommons (CC BY-SA 3.0); 9T kb/WikiCommons (CC BY-SA 3.0); 9B PHGCOM/WikiCommons (CC BY-SA 3.0); 10 Maciej Szczepańczyk/WikiCommons; 11 WikiCommons; 12 Leo Marriott; 13 Pi3.124/WikiCommons (CC BY-SA 4.0); 14T Artwork by Mark Franklin; 14B George Forty Collection; 15 Bundesarchiv Bild 146-1981-147-30A; 16 WikiCommons ; 17 Photo by Szilas in Heeresgeschichtliches Museum/WikiCommons; 18 Leo Marriott; 21T Library of Congress Bain collection; 21B ASM Collection; 22, 23 Leo Marriott; 24T WikiCommons; 24B Leo Marriott; 25 Leo Marriott; 26TL and TR WikiCommons; 26B Frank Vincentz/WikiCommons (CC BY-SA 3.0); 27 Leo Marriott; 28 (both) Leo Marriott; 29 Michael Romagnoli/WikiCommons (CC BY-SA 3.0); 30 BabelStone/WikiCommons (CC BY-SA 3.0); 31T © BrokenSpher /WikiCommons; 31B WikiCommons; 32 Man vyi/WikiCommons; 33T WikiCommons; 33B WikiCommons; 34 (both) Baburnama/WikiCommons; 35 Vssun/Wiki (CC BY-SA 3.0); 36, 37 Air Sea Media collection; 38 Pappenheim/WikiCommons; 39 Adam Jones/WikiCommons (CC BY-SA 3.0); 40L PHGCOM/WikiCommons (CC BY-SA 3.0); 40R Hedwig Bode (CC BY-SA 3.0); 41 PHGCOM/WikiCommons; 42 WikiCommons; 43 PHGCOM/WikiCommons (CC BY-SA 3.0); 44 Pedro J Pacheco/WikiC (CC BY-SA 4.0); 45 Wernervc/WikiCommons (CC BY-SA 4.0); 47TL Yatton at English Wikipedia/WikiCommons; 47TR phaedra/WikiCommons (CC BY-SA 2.0); 47B Lee Sie/WikiC (CC BY-SA 2.0); 48 Simon Cope/WikiC (CC BY-SA 2.0); 49 Holger Weinandt/WikiCommons (CC BY-SA 3.0); 50 Pappenheim/WikiCommons ; 51L Ashwin Kumar/WikiCommons (CC BY-SA 2.0); 51C Prabhavikki (CC BY-SA 3.0); 51R Utpal Basu/WikiCommons (CC BY-SA 3.0); 52 Strahtw/WikiC (CC BY-SA 3.0); 53 Alvesgaspar/WikiC (CC BY-SA 3.0); 54 PHGCOM/Wiki (CC BY-SA 3.0); 55, 56, 57, 58 Library of Congress; 59 Wikipedia Commons; 60 ASM; 61 ASM collection; 62 National Park Service; 63 Fredlyfish4/WikiCommons (CC BY-SA 4.0); 64–65 Acroterion/WikiCommons (CC BY-SA 3.0) (T); U.S. National Park Service (L); Garden_and_Bush_Keys, Alan Schmierer/WikiCommons (C); Library of Congress (R); 66–67 all Library of Congress; 68 Simon Forty; 69 US Army Photo; 70L Library of Congress; 70BR (Source: Flickr Commons project. 2015); 70–71 Parulmah/WikiCommons (CC BY-SA 4.0); 71A NARA; 71B PH2 Paul Soutar/US Navy ; 72L PHGCOM/WikiCommons (CC BY-SA 3.0); 72R PHGCOM/WikiCommons (CC BY-SA 3.0); 73 Leo Marriott; 74 Leo Marriott; 75 WikiCommons; 76 Library of Congress; 77 WikiCommons; 78 Kleon3/WikiC (CC BY-SA 4.0); 79 Library of Congress; 80 NARA; 81–84 all Library of Congress; 85 Brian Stansberry/WikiCommons (CC BY 3.0); 86 NARA; 87, 88 both Library of Congress; 89T Library of Congress; 88B Junglerot56/WikiCommons; 90, 91 both ASM; 92 McKarri/WikiCommons (CC BY-SA 2.0 DE); 93 From Engineering 1880/WikiCommons; 93 inset ShaneCaptHaddockSwartz/WikiCommons; 94, 95 both NARA; 96 WikiCommons; 97, 98, 99 all NARA; 100, 101 both Library of Congress; 102R © Hubertl / WikiCommons (CC BY-SA 4.0); 102L Library of Congress; 103 Library of Congress; 104, 105 NARA; 106 Morio/WikiCommons (CC BY-SA 4.0); 107 AdamAppel/WikiCommons (CC BY-SA 4.0); 108 Bjoertvedt/WikiCommons (CC BY-SA 4.0); 109TL Robert Clark; 109TR WikiCommons; 109B Balcer/WikiCommons (CC BY-SA 3.0); 110, 111 both WikiCommons; 112L Vogl ElemÈr/WikiCommons; 112R WikiCommons; 113 Nikola Smolenski/wikic (CC BY-SA 3.0); 114 NARA; 115 ASM collection; 116, 117 WikiCommons; 118, 119 George Forty collection; © Hubertl/WikiCommons (CC BY-SA 4.0); 121 © Hubertl/WikiCommons (CC BY-SA 4.0); 122, 123 both ASM; 124L WikiCommons; 124R Library of Congress; 125 NARA; 126 George Forty collection; 127 ASM; 128 AMS collection ; 129 NARA; 130 JuFo/WikiCommons (CC

BY-SA 4.0); 131 WikiCommons; 132 Harveyqs/WikiCommons (CC BY-SA 4.0); 133 WikiCommons; 134 George Forty collection; 135 both MKFI/WikiCommons (CC BY-SA 3.0); 136 WikiCommons; 137T US War Dept; 137B ASM; 138 Bibliothèque et Archives Canada/e008315636; 139 Nick-D/WikiCommons (CC BY-SA 3.0); 140L NARA; 140R University de Caen Basse-Normandie/WikiCommons; 141 Library of Congress; 142 ASM collection; 143 WikiCommons; 144, 145 all George Forty collection; 146L Zandcee/WikiCommons (CC BY-SA 3.0); 146R WikiCommons; 147 both Library of Congress; 148T NARA; 148B zongo69/WikiCommons; 149 NARA; 150 Jim.henderson/WikiCommons; 151 US Army Signal Corps; 152T Library of Congress; 152B Mark Pellegrini/WikiCommons (CC-BY-SA-2.5); 153T and BL both NARA; 153BR Library of Congress; 155–159 all NARA; 160T Richieman/WikiCommons; 160B DrAlzheimer/WikiCommons (CC-BY 2.5); 161T www.videgro.net/WikiCommons (CC BY-SA 3.0); 161B Triplph10/WikiCommons (CC BY-SA 4.0); 162 Harold/WikiC (CC BY-SA 3.0); 163 Leo Marriott; 164 NARA; 165 both WikiCommons; 166 US War Dept./WikiCommons; 167 all George Forty collection; 168 George Forty collection;169L Leo Marriott; 169R Bundesarchiv Bild_101I-227-0274-15A; 170 The shaddock/WikiCommons; 171 all NARA; 172 Superx308/WikiCommons; 173 Saiga20K/WikiCommons (CC BY-SA 3.0); 174 George Forty collection; 175T ; 175B Saiga20K/WikiCommons (CC BY-SA 3.0); 176, 177 both ASM collection; 178, 179 both ASM collection; 180 Petr Podebradsky; 181BL Petr Podebradsky; 181TR and BR both NARA; 182 BL Kurt Lund Mogenson; 182TL and BR both Petr Podebradsky; 183 Petr Podebradsky; 184 George Forty collection; 185 Zandcee/WikiCommons; 186 both ASM collection; 187T ASM collection; 187B NARA; 188 ASM; 189 ASM; 190, 191 NARA; 192L Jason Long/WikiCommons (CC BY 3.0); 192TR and BR both NARA; 193–201 NARA; 203 NARA; 204 US Navy photo by Mass Communication Specialist 2nd Class Kristopher Kirsop; 205 Richard Wood; 206, 207 both NARA; 208L NARA; 208R, 209T http://cssbl.com/arsenal/superartilleria_littledavid.htm; 209B NARA; 210–212 NARA; 213 Gandvik/WikiCommons CC BY-SA 3.0; 214 Alf van Beem/WikiCommons; 215 One half 3544/WikiCommons; 216L www.defenceturk.com/; 216R www.defenceturk.com/; 217 WikiCommons (CC BY-SA 3.0); 218 Johnmartindavies/WikiCommons (CC BY-SA 3.0); 219 Simon Cope/WikiCommons (CC BY-SA 2.0); 220 Parutip/WikiCommons (CC BY-SA 3.0); 221 Vitaly V. Kuzmin/WikiCommons (CC BY-SA 4.0)

Index of Weapons